Date Due

MAR 2 8 1973		
JUL 9 1974		
DE 26 '86		
AG 0 5 '77		

Demco 38-299

SOUTH DAKOTA

Here is the story of South Dakota from the time it was a land of swamps and forests, home of the dinosaur, the tiny three-toed horse, and the small pre-historic camel — a land where the Black Hills were ancient before the Alps were born.

The story of the people on the land — of Sitting Bull and Custer, of gold miners at Deadwood, and men riding shotgun on stagecoaches, of Wild Bill Hickok being shot in the back, and settlers breaking the prairie with their plows.

Here is the story of Borglum carving a mountain, and people damming rivers to splash a series of lakes across the state and provide water for dry regions.

Here, in this present home of 28,000 Sioux on 8,000 square miles of reservations, people who have inherited a rich past use the land wisely and face a bright future.

Enchantment of America

SOUTH DAKOTA

By Allan Carpenter

Illustrations by Roger Herrington

CHILDRENS PRESS, Chicago

Consultant
Will G. Robinson, Superintendent,
State Department of History

For their advice and counsel and gracious help, the author thanks:
Nils A. Boe, Governor
Will G. Robinson
South Dakota Educational Association
State Department of Highways
Chamber of Commerce, Rapid City
Public Library, Evanston, Illinois
Tom Balow

Library of Congress Catalog Card Number: 66-10310

2 3 4 5 6 7 8 9 10 11 12 13 14 15 16 17 18 19 20 21 22 23 24 25 R 75 74 73 72 71 70 69 68 67

Contents

A True Story to Set the Scene

Where the Lead Led

"Look what I found!" exclaimed Hattie Foster. In a moment she and George O'Reilly pulled a dirty piece of metal from the ground. The other children who had been playing with her on the gumbo hill near Pierre that Sunday, February 16, 1913, crowded around. They could see that there was some kind of writing on the flat metal, but no one could make it out, and they soon grew tired of it. However, George O'Reilly thought it was lead and might be sold for scrap metal, at the local print shop, so he took it with him.

The metal piece the children had discovered turned out to be one of the historic objects of the continent. The whole account of how it came to be there and the remarkable accident of its recovery make one of the most fascinating of all the stories of enchantment of South Dakota.

One hundred and seventy years before, on March 30, 1743, another group stood on that same hill. These people were the party of the exploring French brothers, François and Louis-Joseph La Vérendrye. They had left French Canada in 1742 trying to find their way to the sea that everyone thought must be not too far to the west. They reached the northern Black Hills before turning back, and on the return trip came to the mouth of the Bad River where it joins the Missouri on March 15, 1743. They had with them a group of the Little Cherry Indians.

The Vérendrye brothers are often said to have been the first Europeans to touch the soil of what is South Dakota, but this now seems doubtful.

While camped on the hill overlooking the Missouri, they buried a lead and zinc plate with a Latin inscription, claiming the region for their king, Louis XV. On the other side, the plate had the following writing in French: "Placed by the Chevalier de La Vérendrye Lo Jost Vérendrye, Louis La Londette A Miotte, The 30th March 1743."

They placed a pile of stones to mark the spot and told the Indians that this was a memorial, since they did not want them to know about the plate. Then they marched on into history. The early settlers in the region found this pile of stones and used it for building materials.

9

The historical facts had been recorded in the Vérendrye journals, but no one ever really expected to see the historic lead plate again. Then George O'Reilly on the way home met two men. They contacted the State Historical Society, suggesting that this might be the missing Vérendrye plate. There was much excitement at the prospect that such a unique historical object might have been re-discovered.

Finally, historians agreed that this must indeed be the long-lost record; the society bought the plate, with Hattie and George sharing the six-hundred dollar purchase price. Today in the Historical Museum of the Memorial Building this storied object may still be seen. More than two-hundred years have passed since the Vérendrye brothers buried it.

In 1933 a monument was dedicated on the hill where the plate had been found, commemorating that memorable, far-off time when the modern history of South Dakota began.

Lay of the Land

Watering the Land

Twenty years ago if anyone had mentioned the Great Lakes of South Dakota he would have been considered slightly unsettled. Yet the course of change and progress was swift in this case. Splashed across the heart of dry central South Dakota today is a series of enormous lakes. These may someday make the region a water playground for untold millions. In an almost unbelievable transformation they have brought the wealth of abundant water to a region where always before it has been the scarcest of natural treasures.

Today South Dakota boasts of two of the world's twelve largest dams — Oahe, just north of Pierre, and Fort Randall, just north of where the Missouri River becomes the Nebraska-South Dakota boundary line. Oahe Dam is the second largest dam in the world, requiring 92,000,000 yards of material in its construction. Fort Randall swallowed up 50,200,000 yards, mostly of earth with some concrete sections, forming Lake Francis Case.

Oahe backs up the waters of the mighty Missouri River for more than half of the distance across the state from north to south to form Oahe Reservoir. The reservoir pushes its sinuous curves far up the valleys of the Cheyenne, Moreau and Grand rivers, covering a total of 23,600,000 acre feet, making it fifteenth in size of all the world's man-made lakes. Other recent gigantic dams are Gavins Point, making Lewis and Clark Lake, and Big Bend, creating Lake Sharpe. Altogether 2,350 miles of new lake shore line have been added recently to South Dakota's resources.

Lake building, on a lesser scale, is not new in South Dakota. Orman Dam, creating Belle Fourche Reservoir, was once the largest earthen dam in the state. Even cities and private individuals have created some of South Dakota's lakes. Lake Mitchell was built by the city of Mitchell. One of the best-known private dams was built in 1891 by Crary and Rede between two giant boulders to create serenely beautiful Sylvan Lake in the Black Hills.

Sand Lake, Columbia, Angostura, and Shadehill are other important reservoirs. Most of the natural lakes are clustered in the lake section of the east and northeast. Among these are Big Stone Lake, Lake Traverse, Waubay, Pickerel, Kampeska, Pelican, Poinsett, Thompson, Oakwood, Herman and Madison. Almost isolated in the southwest is Lacreek Lake. Other lakes include Medicine Lake, taking its name from its medicinal qualities, Legion Lake, known for scenic beauty, and such picturesquely titled lakes as Twin Stink Lakes, Enemy Swim, Blue Dog, Red Iron, and Punished Woman's lakes.

Four South Dakota rivers are found on the United States Geological Survey list of the country's major rivers: The Missouri, Little Missouri, James and Cheyenne. Only a small part of the Little Missouri's length cuts across the northwestern part of South Dakota. Technically, all of the Cheyenne River flows through the state. The James River is often called "the longest non-navigable river in the world." In autumn it becomes almost dry, and in dry seasons it has been known to lose its flow completely. It lies in an old lake bed with a drop of less than 3 inches to the mile across South Dakota. Beginning in North Dakota, the James flows 710 miles to reach the Missouri. No old-timer would recognize the Missouri River as it flows through the state today. The once rampaging, muddy, mighty Mo has been converted into a string of placid lakes. The Missouri's most distinguishing feature in the state — the Big Bend — has been accentuated, and now only a tiny peninsula of land keeps the Bend region from becoming one continuous body of water.

The Big Sioux River forms almost the entire boundary between South Dakota and Iowa. Other rivers are the Vermillion, Moreau, Belle Fourche, Grand, White, and Bad. Fall River is a warm stream which never varies in temperature.

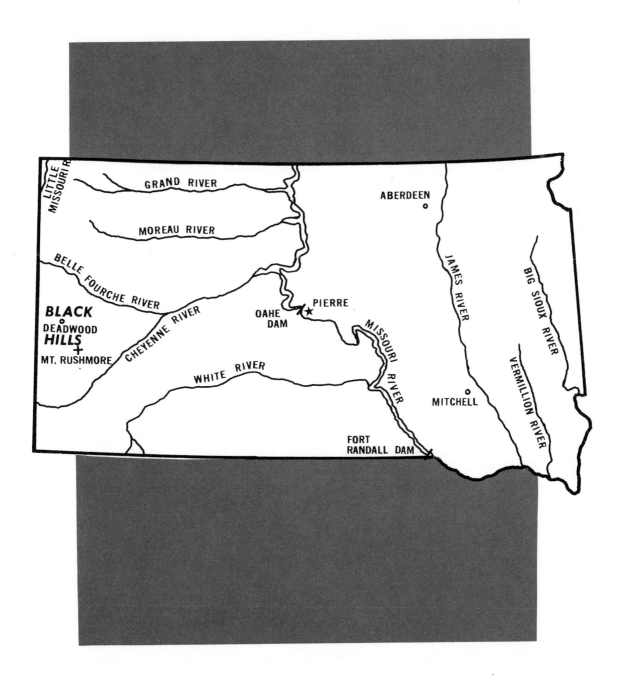

13

In the Dim and Distant Past

One of the world's most interesting areas had its beginnings more than 20,000,000 years ago. The Indians called this region Mako Sico, which means Bad Land, and those who came after them used the same term — Badlands — to describe it. The French translation was *mauvaise terre.* At one time this land was a tropical swamp. Even seas at times covered the region. It was quite different from its high dry nature today. During those millions of years, countless creatures roamed the swamps and forests.

As these died, their remains were covered with silt brought by the many streams. Then throughout the years rain and wind and frost worked on the land to wear it away in great slots, cuts and gashes until now the whole vast area looks like "a part of Hell with the fires burned out," as General George A. Custer described it.

The uncovered bones of so many ancient animals have been found that the Badlands have become known as the world's largest animal graveyard. This makes the Badlands among the most important of all the eroded lands of the world. Possibly more valuable fossils of greater variety have been recovered here than anywhere else. The Badlands have been the most important source of fossils from the Oligocene period — 40,000,000 to 25,000,000 years ago.

It is thought that the camel, at that time unbelievably tiny, originated in the Badlands. Then it migrated to Asia where it grew in size. Although the camel died out in its original home, its small bones have been found in modern times. Bones of the tiny three-toed horse, only 24 inches high, little deer, huge pigs, saber-toothed cats and many other extinct animals, have been uncovered in the Badlands. These can be seen in the School of Mines Museum, Rapid City.

In the breaks of the Missouri and Cheyenne rivers is found shale which once was mud in the bottom of the great Cretaceous sea that was pushed from the area 75 million years ago. In the shale are found fossil remains of fish, turtles, great marine lizards called mosasaurs and plesiosaurs, and millions of fossil shellfish varying from the size of a dime to a Stetson hat. Huge ammonites weighing over a hundred pounds and weird baculites, ancestors of the devil fish, have been

found. These are in especially fine quality and condition.

Fossil Cycad National Monument contains the largest deposits known of the fern-like plants of the Mesozoic period. The fruit of this plant was similar to pineapple. In this same period the dinosaurs roamed the earth and skeletons of these creatures have been found in quantity in South Dakota. King of the dinosaurs, tyrannosaurus rex, brontosaurus, and triceratops have all been recovered in good condition. The Slim Buttes and Hell Creek beds are other renowned sources of fossils.

South Dakota is noted for its many large deposits of petrified wood, covering much of the western part of the state, extending north from the Nebraska border to the largest deposit of all, located in the vicinity of Lemmon. The pieces found range from tiny limbs to huge logs weighing many tons. One of these found near Bison was claimed to be the largest petrified tree in the world. These logs grew possibly a hundred million years ago, were trapped on sandbars in great shallow lakes, covered by soil, turned to stone and then uncovered where they come to light in the present day.

South Dakota's most conspicuous landmarks, the Black Hills, are also relics of ancient times. In fact, they rank among the oldest mountains of the world. They were ancient before the Alps, Pyrenees or Himalayas were yet born.

Untold millions of years ago a great dome of rock, known as a batholith, began to push itself out of the earth over an area about 75 by 150 miles. As the irresistible inner forces moved it ever higher, the batholith shoved aside everything blocking its path. The winds, rains, and frosts of the ages have carved this dome into the Black Hills of today. Because of the extreme hardness of the rock the range has not worn entirely away as so many other mountain masses have done through the eons of time. Actually, some authorities believe that the uplift which formed the Black Hills may still be going on.

The strange formations known as the Needles are the remains of the deepest and oldest rocks pushed up to form the Black Hills. Harney Peak in the Hills is the highest point in the Dakotas — at 7,242 feet.

Admirers of the mythical woodsman Paul Bunyan have another explanation of how the Black Hills came into being. When his beloved blue ox Babe swallowed a red hot stove, it ran bellowing across the prairie but finally died of indigestion and exhaustion. Paul followed and sorrowfully began to pile up a great mound of earth and rocks to bury the animal. This burial mound became the Black Hills. Paul wept as he worked and his tears, so the tale goes, ran together and formed the Missouri River.

One of the most important prehistoric forces responsible for the present land of South Dakota was the glaciers. These great sheets of ice covered the north-central portion of what is now the state and left

16

many marks on the present face of the land. They left rich soil, dotted the countryside with lakes, and deposited mounds of dirt and rock called moraines. The Wessington Hills, a fifty-mile stretch of highlands, are nothing more than a glacial moraine. The hills between Ipswich and Mobridge, swirling like rumpled bedclothes, are also glacially formed.

It is thought that the Missouri River may once have flowed in the James River valley. But pushed out of its old course by the great ice mass, it was forced to make a new route where it flows today — along the western edge of the path of the glacier's farthest reaches.

The Land Today

Although it is only seventeenth in size among the states, South Dakota's 77,047 square miles cover an area larger than all of New England and one and a half times as large as all of England. Meade County, largest in the state, is bigger than Rhode Island and Delaware combined. The state is divided roughly into eastern and western halves by the Missouri River.

The geographical center of South Dakota near Pierre is also the approximate geographical center of the entire North American continent.

One of the continent's watersheds cuts across the northeast corner of the state. Waters falling north of state highway 10 flow to the cold waters of Hudson's Bay and those falling to the south of the highway flow into the Gulf of Mexico. This gives to South Dakota its own kind of a "Continental Divide."

18

The climate is cold in winter and hot in summer, but extreme temperatures are not so common as is often imagined by those not acquainted with the state. The sun shines so much that one of South Dakota's nicknames is the "Sunshine State." The growing season extends from about mid-May through approximately mid-September, although this is less in the Black Hills. Rainfall ranges from about 15 inches per year in the west to around 25 inches in the east.

Some of the country's most noted blizzards have occurred in South Dakota, and two or three severe blizzards may be expected in portions of the state almost every winter. However, they are rarely as severe as the few that have gone down in history because of their unusual tragedies.

Footsteps on the Land

Early Inhabitants

The long line of figures made its way up the hill, each one climbing slowly. Each one struggled to the top and poured dirt from a crude container on the top of a mound at the crest of the hill. When the mound was finished, the workers carefully and laboriously piled rocks on it to form the outline of a giant turtle.

This turtle mound in the Wessington Hills is only one of many mounds found in what is now South Dakota. Little is known about the prehistoric peoples who lived in the region, but it is thought the builders of these mounds were related to those who raised similar mounds found in the more easterly states.

Who they were or how long ago they vanished may never be completely known. Most of what is known about them has been deduced from the objects found in their burial mounds. The early mound builders ate mostly game and made weapons of crude stones. Gradually their implements improved. Finally they passed the stone age and began to use hammered metal. Pottery and personal ornaments have been found. They carefully buried their dead. In spite of the labor required to build the burial mounds with crude digging tools, these were sometimes high enough for many layers of bodies.

Some of the better-known South Dakota mounds are Spirit Mound, north of Vermillion, a group near Sisseton, Sherman Park mounds at Sioux Falls, and Brandon mounds near Sioux Falls, and Hartford Beach on Big Stone Lake.

Carved drawings or petroglyphs, such as those of Cave Hill cliffs, and painted drawings called pictographs, such as those near Flint Hill, are also found in a number of locations. The meaning of these primitive artworks is still unknown.

Earliest inhabitants known to history in what is now South Dakota were the Arikara, commonly known as the Ree Indians. These began in the early 1600's to push their way into the area following the course of the Missouri River. They built villages with circular lodges. One at Fort Sully had over 270 lodges. Lodges were made of sod banked around a framework of poles in the ground, with the upper part finished

in a variety of ways, sometimes with animal skins, sometimes banked with sod or earth.

A buffalo hide covered the hole for the door, and the inside walls were lined with cubicles for sleeping. Up to three families might use one lodge. Most Arikara villages had a large, central council lodge. Usually villages faced a river and were protected by ditches on the other three sides.

BIRD TRACKS

FEASTING

BEAR
TRACKS

SNOWFLAKE

JOY

The Sioux Indians had lived in Wisconsin and Minnesota but they were forced out by the Ojibway, who had guns they bought from the French traders and fur dealers. Beginning about 1750, the Sioux swept into what is now South Dakota from the northeast and after more than fifty years of fighting with the Arikara, the Sioux had almost succeeded in driving the Arikara out of the region. The Sioux word meaning an alliance of friends — *dacotah* — gives the state its name.

The Sioux were governed by tribal councils; they had many chiefs who served more as fathers to their people than as rulers of the tribes. Young men hunted and carried on the war activities. The elders did craft work and carried on the work of the councils. Women raised the simple crops, cared for, processed, transported and stored the food. They made clothing from hides, dressed buffalo skins, and fashioned the tepees of the buffalo hides. Grandmothers were responsible for the care of the children and the instruction of the older girls, while the children carried water and wood, and the boys hunted small game. Girls learned the care, sewing and decoration of skins.

Imaginative designs were worked into clothing, tepees, tobacco bags, moccasins, baby carrying bags and other skin items. Porcupine quills colored with mineral and vegetable dyes were used to make designs. After traders came, Indian craftsmen used beads for their designs. The traditional symbols used in these designs represent ideas such as authority, feasting, life, bear tracks, joy, and other common subjects.

Bows and arrows, pipe stems, ceremonial bowls and other objects were carved crudely with stone implements until knives were available, and then the Indian carving improved greatly.

Medicine men and holy men would retire to such sacred places as the mound overlooking Enemy Swim and Pickerel lakes. Here they would abstain from food and have dreams and visions after days of wailing and chanting. They would interpret these to their people and advise them according to the instructions of their visions.

The Dacotah Indians felt that the dead should be buried high above the ground, and many early settlers told of seeing bodies placed in the lofty branches of such trees as the three sisters cottonwoods at present Pierre.

The people of Mobridge display today two large slabs of rock known as the Conqueror's Stones. In Indian times, chiefs defeated in battle were supposed to have been forced to kneel on the stones with their hands in the hand-shaped grooves to show that they were completely under the control of their captors.

The Indians were greatly concerned with the mysterious and the unusual, especially in nature, and they have many fascinating legends. One of these tells of the boy who became so interested in the sun he would sit and stare at it for hours following its course across the sky. Finally he grew blind from the intense light, but he still sat as he used to and was able by some means to follow the sun across the sky with his blind eyes. When he died and was buried, a straight, tall yellow flower sprang up from his grave. It turned to follow the sun from morning to night. This, said the Indians, was the origin of the sunflower.

An Arikara legend tells of the young brave who was ambushed by the Sioux. Bleeding badly, he tried to run back to warn his friends, staggering and swaying as he ran. In admiration for his bravery, the story says, the Indians piled rocks along the path he ran, a boulder for each drop of his blood. This is said to be the origin of Snake Butte, a long twisting ridge on which today the Center Monument locates the geographical center of the continent.

Another colorful legend tells of the beautiful Indian princess who had many suitors but loved a brave who had gone on a journey. When the other young men insisted she must choose one of them, she said she would marry the one who could throw a great boulder the greatest distance into Lake Kampeska. So many stones were thrown that a small island was formed, but still the girl would not decide. Then the braves marooned her on the island, thinking that she would grow hungry and come to a decision. However, the great white pelicans brought her food, and finally her real lover returned to rescue her. The island is now known as Maiden's Island.

The Dacotah had four main divisions: the Santee, consisting of the Sisiton, Wahpeton, Mdewakanton, and Wahpekute band; the Yankton; the Yanktonnais; and the Teton or Lakota, consisting of the Hunkpapa, Minneconjou, Blackfeet Sioux, Two Kettle, Sans Arc, Brule and Oglala bands.

Wayfarers Pass By

After the Vérendrye brothers left the lead plate as single historic trace of their passing, more than thirty years went by before Pierre Dorion came to live among the Yankton Sioux, about 1780. He married a Sioux woman and became the first white resident of what is now South Dakota. At this time the European settlements on the east coast were already more than two hundred years old.

Jacques d' Eglise was the first St. Louis trader in the area in 1792.

In 1794 schoolteacher Jean Baptiste Trudeau brought ten men from St. Louis and established a trading company. He built Pawnee House, in present Charles Mix County, the first European type structure in the state. Two years later, Registre Loisel built a trading post on an island just above the Big Bend of the Missouri, in present Hughes County, the first permanent fur post.

After the United States bought the Louisiana Territory, America's greatest exploring expedition set out to see what the purchase was like and to gain the Indian's acceptance of the new government. The party led by Meriwether Lewis and William Clark made their first camp in what is now South Dakota at present Elk Point on August 22, 1804 and that night conducted the first election — for sergeant — ever held in the Northwest.

On that date Lewis discovered many minerals and almost died of poisoning while testing some arsenic. The next day they shot in South Dakota the first buffalo they had killed on the trip so far. They investigated Spirit Mound near Vermillion and concluded that the high winds drove many insects to the hill; the birds followed the insects, and the Indians thought the hill was enchanted because of the number of birds there.

Reaching the mouth of the James River on August 27, they made their first contact with the Sioux (the Yankton branch). The Indians, especially the Teton Sioux, had been terrorizing the white traders, forcing them to sell their goods at low prices and not permitting them to go up the Missouri to trade with other Indian tribes upstream. Pierre Dorion, who was guiding the Lewis and Clark travelers, was sent to invite the Yankton to a great feast and council.

At this gathering, Lewis and Clark made efforts to convince the Indians of the wealth and strength of their new government, giving presents and signing treaties of friendship. Knowing how impressed the Indians were with prophecy, Lewis took an Indian baby boy in his arms and wrapped an American flag about him. Solemnly he predicted that this baby would grow up to be a great Indian leader and a fine friend of the Americans. It is interesting to note that the prediction came true. The baby became the powerful Yankton leader named Struck-by-the-Ree and proved his friendship with Americans by saving the settlement of Yankton from an Indian attack.

Lewis made the most thorough, detailed and accurate notes about the Sioux that had ever been taken. They met their first "barking squirrels" — prairie dogs — and found what they thought was a small fox, but they finally decided it was in fact a small wolf — the coyote.

Lewis gave a graphic description of the Dakota prairies: "This plain extends . . . near three miles . . . and it is entirely occupied by the burrows of the barking squirrel . . . in infinite numbers . . . the shortness and verdure of grass gave the plain the appearance throughout its whole extent of beautiful bowling green in fine order. . . . This scenery already rich, pleasing and beautiful was still farther heightened by immense herds of buffalo, deer, elk and antelopes which we saw in every direction feeding on the hills and plains. I do not think I exaggerate when I estimate the number of buffalo which could be comprehended at one view to amount to 3,000."

For four days at present Fort Pierre the party faced a showdown with the Teton Sioux, who tried to keep them from passing; it was one of the major crises they faced on the entire trip. As Ordway, one of the men, reported, "Capt Lewis . . . ordered every man to his arms. The large swivel (cannon) was loaded immediately, the other 2 swivels loaded well with buck shot and each of them manned. Capt Clark used moderation with them, told them that we must and would go on

and would go, that we were not squaws but warriers. The chief sayed
he had warriers too and if we were to go on they would follow us and
kill and take the whole of us. . . . Then Capt Clark told them that we
were sent by their great father the President of the U.S. and that
if they misused us that he or Capt Lewis could be writing to him have
them all destroyed as it were in a moment."

The Teton Sioux were not used to such show of force, and they
backed down. Clark reported: "The great Chief then . . . took up the
pipe of peace . . . lit it and presented the stem to us to smoke . . .
he took . . . some of the most delicate parts of the dog which was prepared for the feast and made a sacrifice to the flag. . . . We smoked for
an hour; 10 musicians playing on tambereens, long sticks with deer
and goats hoofs tied so as to make a gingling noise . . . the women
came forward highly decorated in their way . . . and proceeded to
dance the war dance."

The power of the Teton Sioux after this was never so great, and they
were never quite as much feared as before.

Two years later, the Lewis and Clark party returned down the Missouri River, after the great adventure. Once again they visited the Ree
Indians in the Grand River region as they had on the up-river trip,
but they by-passed the Teton Sioux. They brought with them one of
the great chiefs of the Mandan Indians, Big White.

They had promised Big White safe passage back to his people, and
he returned with a party of soldiers in 1807, but the Ree Indians
attacked the group and killed three of them in the first conflict of
Indians and whites on South Dakota soil.

In 1811 Wilson Price Hunt, agent of John Jacob Astor, led a party
up the Missouri on his way to help establish a fur trading post at far
away Astoria on the Pacific Coast. At the Ree villages he met Manuel

Lisa, a St. Louis fur trader. Lisa was one of the country's great experts on Indians and one of their friends.

The next year Lisa returned to the Dakotas, sent with gifts by William Clark, who was now superintendent of Indian affairs for the Louisiana Territory. His mission was to keep the Indians friendly during the War of 1812. He built Fort Manuel, and when this was destroyed by the Indians, he built a second fort at Big Bend. The work of Lisa among the Indians was especially helpful in holding the West for America during and after the war.

Permanent Beginnings

Joseph La Framboise established a fort at the mouth of the Bad River in 1817. In 1822 the Columbia Fur Company built nearby Fort Tecumseh. In 1831 this was replaced by Fort Pierre Chouteau, finally shortened to Fort Pierre. This is the oldest continuously inhabited settlement in what is now South Dakota.

General William Ashley visited the Ree village with a trading party in 1823. At Ashley Island his party was caught in a surprise attack, with a number killed. Jedediah Smith, who later became a noted frontiersman, offered prayers for the wounded, and this is believed to be the first religious service on South Dakota soil. As punishment for the attack, the Ree Indians were driven out of South Dakota by Colonel Henry Leavenworth, and they never returned to the state.

Fur trading continued to be the main occupation of the region. In 1835 the American Fur Company built a trading post on the banks of the Missouri River near present Vermillion. The exact site of this post was washed away by the river. Another trading post was established on Elm River north of what is now Aberdeen in 1836. Already the convenient transportation of the steamboat had come to the region. The first of the "puffing canoes," the *Yellowstone,* had reached Fort Pierre in 1831.

On his explorations of 1838 and 1839, John C. Frémont, the "Pathfinder," explored parts of what is now South Dakota, mapping, tracing the water levels and achieving other scientific "firsts" in the area.

The first sermon in the Dakotas was preached by the Reverend Stephen R. Riggs at Fort Pierre in 1840, and the first mass was celebrated in 1842 on the James River in Brown County, by Father A. Ravoux. Father Christian Hoecken baptised many half-breed children along the Missouri in 1840. The famed explorer-priest-missionary, Father Peter John DeSmet, visited South Dakota in 1848. In the Black Hills an Indian chief offered him as a gift a bag of glittering powder, probably stolen from a scalped prospector. Recognizing it for gold, Father DeSmet refused the gift and said, "It rouses the passions of some white men. Put it away and show it to nobody." This was many years before gold was known definitely in the Hills.

The Government bought Fort Pierre from its private owners in 1855.

Two years later the Indian renegade, Inkpaduta, brought the captives of his Spirit Lake, Iowa, massacre into what is now South Dakota. He held his hostages at what is now Lake Herman near Madison. At Lake Thompson a group of Santee Sioux caught up with Inkpaduta. In a fierce battle two of the gangster Indian's sons were killed, but he escaped. One of the most famous of all Indian captives was thirteen-year-old Abigail Gardner, abducted from her Spirit Lake home and tortured unmercifully. She was finally freed near present Ashton through the efforts of the missionaries Williamson and Riggs and three of their Christian Indians.

In the same year, 1857, another event was the mapping and exploration of the Black Hills by Lieutenant G. K. Warren of the Army, who made the first detailed report on that mysterious mountain range.

On March 2, 1861, President James Buchanan signed the papers creating Dakota Territory, including all of what is now North and South Dakota and Montana, plus the northern two-thirds of Wyoming and part of Nebraska. In this entire huge region only 2,402 people were living at the time. Abraham Lincoln proceeded to organize the territory when he became President, with the capital at Yankton and Dr. William Jayne of Springfield as first territorial governor.

Because of the small population, South Dakota took no part in the Civil War, but enough men volunteered to provide two companies of Dakota Cavalry which was used for protection against the Indians. In 1862 the Santee Sioux began an uprising known as the War of the Outbreak. Only one skirmish of this war took place in South Dakota, occurring in a hayfield outside of present Sioux Falls.

An interesting occurrence of this war was the rescue of white captives by a group of eleven young Indian men. They had taken an oath to help the whites and for this reason were given the nickname of the Fool Soldier Band. To ransom the prisoners, held near present Mobridge, they traded away almost everything they had except one horse and two guns.

The War of the Outbreak was settled in 1865 at a great council with the Indians at old Fort Sully just east of present Pierre.

Let's Get Settled

January 1, 1863, was one of the most significant dates in the history of South Dakota. The Homestead Act took effect on that date. Under this act homesteaders could claim 160 acres of land by meeting certain conditions. The principal one of these conditions was that they must live on their property for a specified time in order to receive title to it.

South Dakota had the honor of the first homestead claim in the United States — registered by Mahlon Gore on land near Elk Point. From that time on a steady stream of homesteaders plodded across the territory on the way to find the property of their dreams. Where trees were available, log houses were built. Sod shanties began to blossom on the prairies where there were no trees. These were crude shelters, partly underground. Blocks of the prairie sod, held together by a network of roots, were cut five-inches thick and used for the walls of these pioneer dwellings. Chinks were filled with a mortar of damp earth. Roofs were supported by scattered limbs or brush covered with a layer of dirt. It was a hard and lonely life, but few complained.

Certain improvements were required before a homesteader could receive his land patent. One of these was the plowing of a certain amount of land. When one rather lazy homesteader was asked how much acreage he had plowed, he replied, "Around twenty." When his story was checked it was found that he had plowed one furrow "around" twenty acres of land.

Fort Sisseton was established in 1864. Supplies had to be carried more than 240 miles from St. Paul. Much of the building stone was dragged across the prairies from as far as Wahpeton, North Dakota. Fort Sisseton cost $2,000,000 to build — almost unheard of at that time for a pioneer military installation. As time went by, the fort became the center for social and cultural activities for the entire half of the state.

Another important event came in 1865. Building of Fort Dakota began the first in a long series of developments still going on in the Sioux Falls area.

The year 1865 saw a plague of grasshoppers and also brought another Indian disturbance. Chief Red Cloud of the Oglala Sioux was disturbed by the fact that the buffalo hunting grounds were faced with destruction by the settlers, and he went on the warpath, winning a series of brilliant victories over the Army. This is said to be the only time in history when the Army was defeated by an equal force of Indians. This powerful chief demanded that the government abandon all its forts in a large area and leave the region entirely to the Indians. Finally a treaty was signed in which the United States agreed to give up its forts and keep all settlers from a vast region between the Big Horn Mountains on the west, the Missouri River on the east and the north, and the Niobrara River on the south. This was to be a permanent hunting ground for the Indians, and the treaty could never be changed without the consent of 75 per cent of all the braves of the region. The Black Hills were to remain for all time the sacred place of the Indians — home of the Great Spirit.

G-o-l-d!

The government wasted little time in breaking this solemn agreement with the Indians. In 1874 General George Armstrong Custer was sent into the Black Hills with one of the largest military expeditions in the history of the West. The party included 1,200 men, 110 wagons, six ambulances, and several field cannon, drawn by six mules apiece. Three hundred beef cattle followed the wagon train to supply meat. The tracks of the wagons can still be seen in some places. Interesting old photographs of the expedition show it covering the prairie as far as the eye could see.

This was to be a scientific expedition to discover what minerals were there and to study the geology of the region. The party moved from Wyoming into present South Dakota, marveling at the beautiful meadows of flowers and cool clear streams they passed on the way. Camping on the headwaters of French Creek, Custer climbed Harney Peak; there is no record of any earlier climb of this mountain.

More important, however, while at this camp, one of the party, Horatio N. Ross, in late July or early August, discovered gold about three miles east of the present location of the town of Custer. One authority has called this the "most important single event in South Dakota history."

News of the discovery was sent back to Custer's superior, General Phil Sheridan, in St. Louis by one of the Custer scouts, Charlie Reynolds. The camp blacksmith nailed the shoes backwards on Reynolds' horse so that the tracks would confuse the Indians. However, the Indians kept entirely away from the Custer expedition.

No one knows how the gold discovery news reached a Chicago newspaper, but even before Custer's messenger came to General Sheridan, a Chicago paper's headlines read, "GOLD! The Land of Promise! Stirring News From the Black Hills! The Glittering Treasure! Found at Last — A Belt of Gold Territory 30 Miles Wide! The Precious Dust Found Under the Horses' Feet! Excitement Among the Troops!"

Before the day was over the first floods of gold seekers were already setting out for the Black Hills. South Dakota would never be the same again.

31

Yesterday and Today

Changing the Unchangeable

Before the end of 1874, a high log stockade and cabins had been built by the "Gordon Party," led by John Gordon, almost on the exact spot where Ross found his gold before. They spent the winter there without trouble from the Indians; other miners straggled in. They called the new community Custer, in honor of the handsome, yellow-haired general. Then they were removed by the government since they violated the treaty with the Indians.

Nevertheless, in spite of governmental restrictions, thousands of gold seekers began to gather on the boundaries waiting for some means of getting in to gold country. Hundreds, probably thousands, slipped in illegally. The government offered the Indians $6,000,000 for the Black Hills, but the offer was turned down with indignation. Finding the task almost impossible, the Army gave up trying to keep prospectors out of the Hills. By mid-December, 1875, Custer had a population of 10,000 and boasted 2,700 structures.

Then in late 1875 James Pearson, a Yankton prospector, discovered gold in the northern Black Hills in a gulch where many of the trees were dead. By early spring 1876 the rush began to Dead Tree Gulch, which came to be known as Deadwood. Custer became, for a while, practically a ghost town almost as soon as it was born. Men were digging for gold everywhere. By mid-summer of 1876, there were more than 25,000 people in Deadwood Gulch, and the town of Deadwood was laid out. All of these people were squatters on Indian land.

The Indians were appalled at this invasion and tearing up of their sacred lands in violation of solemn treaties. Many miners lost their scalps in swift attacks by Indian bands.

Greatest disaster of the period, of course, was the battle of Little Big Horn in Montana, where General Custer's carelessness cost him his own life and that of all his troops.

General George Crook met the Indians in the small battle of Slim Buttes in what is now Harding County. He burned an Indian village nearby. In returning from this battle, Crook's cavalry forces crossed the South Dakota gumbo country, where wet mud "gums" up on the feet of men and animals until it is almost impossible to walk. General Crook reported that probably there had never been more hardship and suffering in the history of the army.

Although the Indians had won some success, it was apparent that they could not hold out long against the growing power of the army. In the fall of 1876 a peace commission negotiated a new treaty turning over the Black Hills to the settlers. However, later the Indians claimed this included only mineral rights, not title to the land itself.

A Rip-roaring Time

As Deadwood grew, so did its reputation for being one of the most rootin'-tootin'-shootin' towns of the entire old West. Almost every famous lawman and outlaw of the West found his way there at one time or another. The well-known or picturesque characters who walked Deadwood streets included Wyatt Earp, Wild Bill Hickok, Calamity Jane, Sam Bass, Potato Creek Johnny Perret, California Joe, and a host of others.

Regular stage lines were established out of the Hills, and for a while they got along well, but in March, 1877, Sam Bass held up a stage bringing currency to the Deadwood banks. Popular Johnny Slaughter, the driver, was killed. From that time on, it seemed that hardly a stage got through without a holdup. A typical report of the Deadwood *Pioneer* read: "The Fort Pierre stage was held up again last night. The road agents got $460 from the passengers and $5,000 in gold dust — the cleanup of the Midas No. 2 Gold Mine."

It became necessary to send "shotgun messengers" in an armored "treasure coach" whenever valuable shipments were being made. The richest load of gold sent out of the Black Hills was worth $200,000. Wyatt Earp rode shotgun on this shipment, and his reputation was so great that the gold got through without trouble. Another of the best-known treasure guards was Scott Davis.

Whenever an outlaw, robber or suspected criminal was captured, his immediate future became very uncertain. Vigilantes were apt to hang a suspect to the nearest tree and inquire afterward into his guilt.

Deadwood itself was a rip-roaring town. Shootings and brawls were so common they attracted little notice. One shooting, however, drew the attention of the whole world. James Butler Hickok (Wild Bill) had

become probably the best-known figure in the West. As a lawman he had cleaned up some of the most notorious towns in the country. When he came to Deadwood he was thought by some to be a terrible, quick-on-the-trigger villain. Others considered him a knight in shining armor.

Actually, Hickok was quite generally respected by those who knew him. He had a fearsome reputation for his ability with a gun, but no one had ever proved that he shot in anything but self-defense. He was a handsome, well-built man with gentlemanly, almost quiet manners.

When Hickok went into a saloon called Number Ten in Deadwood on August 2, 1876, to take his usual place at the poker table, he found Charlie Rich sitting in it, as Charlie said "just to plague him." So Wild Bill, forgetting his usual caution, sat down with his back to the door. Into the bar sauntered an unprepossessing character named Jack McCall. He bought a drink then strolled to the door. Not more than two feet behind Wild Bill, McCall suddenly drew his gun and shot Hickok in the head.

Thousands of people passed by the casket where Wild Bill's body lay in state, dressed in a new suit, starched shirt and flowing black tie, with his favorite rifle lying beside him; almost all of Deadwood followed him to his grave.

Deadwood had no regular courts at that time, but Jack McCall was arrested and found not guilty in one of the strangest "trials" on record. Later he stood trial in Yankton, was convicted and hanged. No one ever knew the reason why he murdered the West's best-known character.

Meanwhile, Deadwood grew and prospered. In 1879 the wooden town was destroyed by fire, but quickly rebuilt. This time the buildings were sturdy, permanent structures. Many of them have lasted to the present day, giving the city a "pioneer" appearance.

Hardships to Overcome

As the great drama of gold in the Hills was being played, the rest of the region was not idle. Communities were springing up, and people were battling the strong forces of Nature to survive on the prairies.

In the winter of 1880-1881 the country suffered the worst storms in its history, and the people of South Dakota endured terrible hardships.

Heavy snows fell in October; one of the blizzards during the year was the worst on record, and snows continued well into the spring.

When the snows finally melted, awful floods occurred. An ice dam formed in the Missouri River near Yankton; the river was full of ice as far as Springfield, thirty miles away. Suddenly the ice dam broke sending untold forces of ice and water hurtling downstream. Steamboats at docks were smashed; people hastened to high ground to watch all their belongings being swept away. The entire village of Green Islands was destroyed. The story was told that the church was swept away and floated downstream intact. People down river reported seeing this ghostly "craft" sail by and heard the eerie sound of the church bell. Fortunately, few lives were lost but property damage was frightful throughout the young countryside.

In 1888 another blizzard, although not quite so bad as that of 1881, took more lives because of the increased population. The temperature shot down 70° in a few hours. Winds of more than 60 miles per hour drove snow like steel pellets into the faces of those caught in the storm that came with almost no warning. Those who were killed were found as they had fallen, some propped against haystacks, some with knees drawn up in a desperate effort to keep warm. A hundred and seventy-four persons in South Dakota lost their lives in that storm.

Prairie fires were another dread of early settlers. The strong prairie winds would fan a fire in the long grasses until it swept across the open land like the torrent of a volcano, wiping out many a farm home in a shower of pitiful sparks.

Life as a State

By 1889 the Dakotas were ready to become states. The ceremony of statehood was one of the most interesting and unusual in our history. President Benjamin Harrison prepared to sign the statehood documents for both North and South Dakota. To keep one state from claiming precedence over the other, the President hid the documents from the onlookers. He never disclosed the secret as to which one he signed first. No one knows to this day which was the 39th and which the 40th state. Generally the two states are listed in rank according to the alphabet. This kind of arrangement makes North Dakota the 39th and South Dakota the 40th.

36

Arthur C. Mellette, last governor of the territory, was elected to serve as the first governor of South Dakota as a state.

By a strange chance, South Dakota became the final stage for one of the greatest dramas in United States history which had been running for a period of over three hundred years — the titanic struggle with the Indians.

The last Indian struggle of any consequence began with a Nevada Indian, Wovoka, who became known as the Messiah. Wovoka claimed he had seen visions in which the buffalo were restored, the whites driven out and the glory of the Indians returned to the land. The cult of the Messiah spread rapidly among the Indians across the West. They danced the strange ghost dance, whirling and gyrating crazily until they dropped from exhaustion. They put on a calico "ghost shirt" and thought they were able to withstand the white man's bullets.

Late in 1890 the Sioux began to gather along the Cheyenne River. Sitting Bull, who defeated General Custer, was wrongly believed responsible for the unrest. Indian policemen of his own tribe, representing the government, were sent to arrest him at his village on Grand River, west of where present Little Eagle stands. He agreed to go with them and sent for his horse, the favorite trick horse he had ridden in Buffalo Bill's Wild West Show. After leaving his tent, Sitting Bull suddenly called out "I'm not going," and his angry followers closed in. During the struggle that followed between 43 police and 150 warriors of Sitting Bull, the old medicine man and chief was killed.

One of the strangest actions of this battle was the behavior of Sitting Bull's horse. As the fighting raged he calmly went through the routine of tricks he had learned in the circus. This struck terror in many of the superstitious Indians who were fighting.

After the death of Sitting Bull many of his band went to the village of Chief Big Foot, who moved into the Badlands and south into the Pine Ridge Reservation. Here they were discovered by a strong cavalry force, to whom they surrendered. The Indians were taken to a point on Wounded Knee Creek, where they were surrounded by a strong force who insisted that they give up all remaining guns. Big Foot was dying of pneumonia and was unable to assert any leadership. Yellow Bird and other medicine men urged the men of the village to

37

resist the soldiers, claiming the Indians could never be killed because they were protected by their ghost shirts. Shots were fired, by whom no one knows, and soon there was a melee of indiscriminate firing. The troops had Hotchkiss guns, an early type of machine gun, and the tragedy of Wounded Knee became a massacre of the Indians. This inexcusable action was laid to the fact that the troops were inexperienced. Thirty-one soldiers lost their lives and 146 Indians were killed, including Big Foot and his son. The Messiah War had come almost to an end.

This was the last large scale military action ever to take place between whites and Indians in the United States.

In another war, the Spanish-American, South Dakota raised and equipped a regiment of volunteers to fight in the far away Philippines, and several South Dakota men received Congressional Medals of Honor.

"Battles" of another kind took part in many places in the state. This was the long continuing struggle over county seats. Whenever a new county seat was to be selected, rival towns could be depended upon to struggle fiercely to win the prize.

An example of these arguments was the trouble that occurred in Spink County. Redfield had been elected as the county seat, but Ashton kept the records, until a group from Redfield slipped quietly into Ashton and stole the records. Then an "army" of about 1,500 men descended on Redfield; Redfield citizens hired a locomotive, went to Milbank and got a court injunction to keep the county records. Perhaps this injunction was the only thing that kept the dispute from turning into a real battle. In any event, the county seat remained at Redfield.

In another of these struggles both Clear Lake and Gary built splendid courthouses to attract the county seat of Deuel County. When Clear Lake won, the Gary building eventually became the State School for the Blind.

An even fiercer argument had taken place during many years about the location of the state capital. Pierre had been elected the capital in 1889 and 1890, but Mitchell got the 1903 legislature to reopen the issue. The North Western Railroad supported Pierre, and the Milwaukee Railroad helped Mitchell. The railroads carried almost 100,000 people on free passes to visit the two rival cities. In the election of 1904, Pierre again won, and the legislature provided for a permanent capitol building there.

During World War I, South Dakota sent 32,791 of her citizens into the service of their country. It is interesting to note that South Dakota men had the finest health record of any state among the first groups drafted for service for that war.

In 1919 the first public bridge across the Missouri River in South Dakota was begun at Yankton, where the citizens had raised money for it.

World attention turned to South Dakota in 1927 in a way it never had before. Governor Carl Gunderson sent a formal invitation to President Calvin Coolidge to spend the summer in the Black Hills, and the President accepted. The President enjoyed his summer White House in the state game lodge. A special golf course had been built for him, and it was rumored that all the greens slanted toward the hole.

The world marveled at the President's skill as a fisherman. William Bulow, who succeeded Governor Gunderson, later revealed how he made the President "the greatest fisherman since Isaac Walton." The governor had workmen fence off a three-mile section of Squaw Creek near the game lodge. He stocked this part of the stream with fish that were veteran pets of the state fish hatchery at Spearfish. Most of their lives they had been fed ground meat. After a week in the unfamiliar stream where they were unable to find anything to eat, the pet trout were ready to strike at anything, and the President had a grand time; he never knew how he acquired his new-found fishing skill.

One night the President invited Governor Bulow to dinner. The Governor was dismayed to find his plump, oily, almost uneatable trout on the menu. "I caught them myself," the President declared proudly. The President enjoyed the dark, quiet beauty of the Hills so much he delayed his stay long after the planned time to depart.

Mr. Coolidge posed for countless pictures in cowboy hats, chaps and the headdresses of Indian chiefs. He visited the Black Hills Roundup and promoted other local attractions. Many were surprised that he appeared to be a quite satisfactory horseman. It must certainly be said that the tremendous amount of publicity that came from South Dakota during the long summer "put the Black Hills on the map."

History on a Mountain

Climax of Mr. Coolidge's visit came on August 10, 1927, when he rode horseback up a hot and dusty gully with an escort of cavalry followed by hundreds of perspiring people staggering on foot up the mountainside, including the Governor, newspapermen and newsreel cameramen.

The occasion was the dedication of what was then hoped to be a memorial. But many people had strong doubts that it ever would take form. In his dedication speech Mr. Coolidge said, "This memorial will crown the height of land between the Rocky Mountains and the Atlantic seaboard, where coming generations may view it for all time . . . We have come to dedicate a cornerstone that was laid by the hand of the Almighty. On this towering wall . . . is to be inscribed a memorial which will represent some of the outstanding events of American history . . ." Those who heard the President on that occasion said it was the finest speech he had ever made.

The occasion, of course, was the dedication of Mount Rushmore as the site of the world's mightiest sculpture. Two or three years earlier state historian Doane Robinson had interested famed sculptor Gutzon Borglum in carving a gigantic statue on one of the Black Hills. The sculptor crawled over many possible sites before selecting Mt. Rushmore, which was then not even reached by roads. Contributions began to come in from school children, business firms, and many others. Almost the last official act of Calvin Coolidge as President was to sign a law creating the Rushmore National Memorial Commission giving a federal appropriation for the project.

No chisel and hammer would do for this enormous work. Great quantities of dynamite had to be used to remove huge masses of granite. Sculptor Borglum became so skillful that he could dynamite to within two inches of what would be the finished surface of his figure. If these figures included whole persons instead of just heads, they would be at least 465 feet tall. The sculptor created such perfect likenesses that there is no distortion no matter from what angle they are viewed. This is particularly remarkable when it is remembered that the sculptor could never get any view of what he was doing when he was at the sculpture itself. The heads are so large it is possible to stand in Jefferson's eye.

While the carving went on, some remarkable roads were being built to reach the monument. When making a tunnel on one of these roads, the workmen broke through the rock and found that the memorial was perfectly framed in the tunnel mouth. Two more of these remarkable "windows" were then made purposely, helping to make the drive to the memorial one of the most unusual anywhere.

The figure of George Washington was dedicated in 1930. President Franklin D. Roosevelt dedicated the Thomas Jefferson figure in 1936. Abraham Lincoln's head was dedicated in 1937, and the head of Theodore Roosevelt was dedicated in 1939. In 1941 Gutzon Borglum died of a heart attack, and the work was carried on by his son Lincoln. Actually the Rushmore Memorial was never finished; work stopped when the money ran out in 1941. However, few people miss the refining touches that might have been placed on Roosevelt's tie, Lincoln's lapel or other features. Few visitors can gaze at this extraordinary accomplishment without a feeling of awe and considerable reverence.

As sculptor Borglum said, "I want . . . a few feet of stone that carries the likenesses, the dates, a word or two of the great things we accomplished as a Nation, placed so high that it won't pay to pull it down for lesser purposes . . . to show posterity what manner of men our leaders were. Then breathe a prayer that these records will endure until the wind and the rain alone shall wear them away." Most people will agree that he accomplished what he set out to do.

The Troublesome Thirties

Depression and lack of rain made the hard times of the thirties especially difficult in South Dakota. Four years of relentless drought from 1933 through 1936 brought choking dust storms and ruin for many farmers and ranchers. Clouds of dust darkened the sun; drifts of topsoil piled up behind fences and covered farm machinery; people gasped for breath.

In desperation, people turned to "rainmakers" who said they could bring rain with machines and chemicals. The Sioux revived their rain dance, after considerable difficulty because no one could remember how it went. Finally, of course, the rains did come again. For more permanent relief, the federal government planted thousands of trees in shelter-belts to help keep the wind from blowing the topsoil away.

The winter of 1935-1936 added further to the hardships by being one of the snowiest and coldest on record.

South Dakota had a peculiar distinction during the "bank holiday" proclaimed by President Franklin D. Roosevelt to help overcome the losses of bank failures. Al Nystrom's bank at Wall was the only bank in the country which operated throughout the bank holiday. No one had thought to notify Mr. Nystrom, and he was not aware that he was supposed to close.

Not all the news of the thirties was bad. The 1933 change in the price of gold brought a renewal of gold mining in the Black Hills, and the Hills gained another of their many distinctions in 1935 when the huge balloon *Explorer II* rose slowly into the dawn out of the Stratosphere Bowl. In these days of space flight the record of 13.71 miles in the stratosphere set by *Explorer II* does not seem very high, but it was an incredible achievement for its time. The balloon and its crew, Albert W. Stevens and Orvil A. Anderson, landed safely at White Lake after more than eight hours.

In 1939 President Roosevelt proclaimed the Badlands as a National Monument.

In World War II, 64,560 men and women from South Dakota were members of the armed services.

The Modern State and Its People

The recent history of South Dakota is concerned mostly with developments such as building the great Missouri River dams and creating their enormous lakes, the growth of tourist trade, expansion of roads and communications, progress of industry and other modern concerns. These are covered in more detail in other sections of this book.

And what of the people of South Dakota who possess the present and have inherited the past?

Many languages, cultures and ethnic groups have contributed to the present-day population. Groups of Germans, Finns, and other Scandinavians still keep the language, home life, cooking, and other customs of the homeland, although they are perfectly at home with the English language and modern day life.

The German-Russians at Aberdeen and Rockport, Swiss at Legia Greischa Colony near Arlington, Norwegians at Baltic (Little Norway), Swedish people of Beaver Valley, the Chinese of Deadwood — all and many more have contributed to the life of the state. At one time it was estimated that there were eighteen different nationalities working in the mines of Lead alone.

The state's original settlers also are very much a part of life in the state today. There are 28,000 Indians in modern South Dakota, mostly of Sioux descent. The major reservations — Pine Ridge, Rosebud, Cheyenne River, Lower Brule, and Crow Creek — contain 8,400 square miles of land.

Artist David Miller, who painted many portraits of older Indian leaders, said, "I have learned to like the Sioux best of the Indian tribes. . . . Despite all that has been done to them they are still a fine, upstanding race of people who have had a glorious past and certainly deserve a better future. . . . The Sioux, once the most warlike, are now the friendliest of the Indian tribes."

Almost two hundred and twenty-five years ago, when the Indians of South Dakota had seen only a few white men, an Indian medicine man named Tasonkesapa made one of the remarkable prophecies of history. He said he had asked the Great Spirit about the meaning of these strangers. "The Great Spirit answered," Tasonkesapa said, " 'The buffalo and wild things will disappear.' "

The old things have indeed disappeared to a large extent. However, both the Indians and their neighbors probably would agree that, working together, they have built an even better world of today in the state they both love.

Natural Treasures

Brahmalos, Cattalos, and Other Animals

A group of beavers watched in 1937 as engineers built a dam across Deer Creek not far from Savoy. The engineers may have thought the beavers were interested in learning new construction methods. However, the beavers were really trained technical observers. After several days of careful study, they went about half a mile upstream and built a new house. When the dam was finished and the lake filled up, their new house was situated exactly where beavers like to have their houses. Somehow those animal engineers knew that their old house would be flooded; they knew exactly what kind of dam the men were building and exactly where the water level would come throughout the new lake.

Beavers and other fur bearers provided most of the early business in what is now South Dakota — as white merchants traded beads, blankets, guns, ammunition and other items the Indians wanted for the valuable fur pelts collected by the braves.

Once the most important animal in the area, providing the Indians with a large part of their food, clothing, and shelter, the buffalo lives today only in protected herds in South Dakota. However, the herd in Custer State Park is the largest in the country. The last of the country's great wild herds of buffalo were killed in an awful slaughter in the Camp Crook region. A mystery of Nature is the reason for the great mound of thousands of buffalo bones found buried beneath the earth near Lemmon. No one has been able to explain how so many of these animals long ago met their deaths in such a small area.

Experiments with buffalo in South Dakota in recent years have created such unusual beasts as the cattalo, part cattle and part buffalo, and the brahmalo, part brahma cattle and part buffalo.

It is estimated that there are 30,000 antelope in the state, largely in the northwest. South Dakota State Antelope Preserve is the only place where these animals are reared in captivity.

Elk, deer, mountain goats, coyotes, a host of smaller animals, and even a herd of wild burros in Custer State Park add to the interest of hunters and nature lovers in the state.

CANVASBACK DUCK

RING-NECKED PHEASANT

WHITE PELICAN

Feathers and Scales

In 1898 the ringnecked pheasant was introduced into South Dakota; this immigrant did so well that now it is the state bird, and South Dakota is known as the "Pheasant Capital of the World," with a pheasant population estimated at over 10,000,000 beauties. The approach of pheasant hunters to the state during the season is almost a stampede.

Another popular South Dakota bird, the wild duck, received his colorful iridescent plumage in South Dakota, according to Indian legend. A young brave sat down on the shore of Rush Lake one day. He loved bright colors and had been collecting the colored minerals and dye plants of the region to make his paints. The water birds came to the shore of the lake and complained that they were too drab and dull; they asked him to color their feathers. So he started out, worked as fast as he could, and managed to cover all his friends except the goose and the loon. Then his colors ran out, and those two birds have remained forever as they were, while the others have bright feathers.

Another popular South Dakota bird for hunting is the Hungarian partridge. Many visitors are astonished to see great white pelicans so far inland, and the many cormorants on Cormorant Island on Waubay Lake are also a surprise to some.

Altogether, almost 300 species of birds have been found in South Dakota, including the water ouzel, prairie chicken, blackbirds, flickers, goldfinch, kingfisher, humming birds, catbirds, bluebirds, thrushes, wrens, warblers, crossbills, eagles, magpies, buzzards, owls and hawks.

Trout in great numbers flock to the fishermen's bait in the Black Hills, and the flashing finny prizes constantly are added in good supply from some of the nation's finest hatcheries, such as that at Spearfish.

On and Under the Ground

One of the world's largest deposits of bentonite is found near Belle Fourche. Two-hundred-and-fifty different types of minerals are found in the Black Hills alone. In the region of Keystone are found 87 types — more minerals than found in any area of similar size in the world. These include beryl, pollucite, andalusite, lapidolite, phosphate, and arsenic. Innumerable gem stones are found in the state, including emeralds, rubies and sapphires. The state is noted for the enormous size of its pegmatite crystals, including beryllium.

Oil exploration holds out great promise of petroleum riches. Uranium, mica, beryl, manganese, corundum, feldspar, limestone and other building stone, sand and gravel, and coal are all important. The lignite fields of Harding County alone are estimated to contain a billion tons of that type of coal. Gold, of course, remains a stand-by.

Total resources for hydroelectric power have hardly been calculated yet, and the water of the artesian basin in central South Dakota is of great importance.

Stands of ponderosa pine account for 98 per cent of the forested lands of the Black Hills, providing the dark green color that from a distance makes them look almost black, giving the Hills their name. Limber and lodgepole pine, cedar, spruce, juniper, aspen, balsam, poplar, birch, burroak, hackberry, willow and ash are other trees of the state. The cottonwood, which will grow in dry areas where no other trees are found, has long been a favorite of settlers.

Many cottonwoods have been landmarks for large regions. The "Lone Tree" near Flandreau was such a landmark. When engineers decided to cut it down for highway construction, protests from all over the country poured in, but the tree was not saved.

First flower of the spring is the state flower, the delicate light purple pasqueflower, much loved by the people of the state. Primrose and wild rose, lilies of the lakes and creeks, blazing stars, wild geranium, prickly poppy, gumbo lily are other wildflowers. A surprising number of cacti are found, sometimes blanketing the western hills with spring bloom. Yucca also is plentiful. Black Hill flowers include woodland star, larkspur, monkshood, fleur-de-lis, yellow lady slipper, bluebell, wood orchid, baby's breath, shooting star, and sunflower.

49

People Use Their Treasures

"That Home Stake You Were Looking For"

In 1949 South Dakota became the nation's greatest gold producing state and has held that position continually ever since. This is not surprising. During its history the Homestake Mine at Lead has alone produced more gold than any other single mine in the world. The South Dakota gold discovery helped to overcome the depression of 1873. Almost half a billion dollars of gold has come from South Dakota since the discovery of 1874, most of that from the Homestake — now the only major gold producer operating in the United States.

In April, 1876, Fred Manuel and his brother Moses, a veteran prospector, made a strike in Gold Rush Gulch. Fred remarked, "This looks like that home stake you were looking for so long." He could not have been more right. Later, one of the world's leading mining figures, George Hearst, founder of the famous Hearst fortune, became interested in Manuel's discovery. With Hearst backing, the Homestake Company was properly organized and in less than a year began its continually successful operation. The town of Lead was established. Lead (rhymes with seed) takes its name from the mining term meaning vein or lode.

Since its beginning, the Homestake has opened up over 200 miles of tunnels containing almost 100 miles of narrow-gauge railroad. Its open pit mine forced the town of Lead to retreat many times as the pit engulfed more and more of the territory. The cost and size of the operation can be seen by the fact that when all the processes have been completed, an entire ton of raw ore yields only 33 ounces of gold.

After gold, in order of their value, South Dakota produces the following minerals: sand and gravel, stone, cement, uranium, and clays for a total annual mineral value of $51,000,000 as of 1964.

Most of the clay value comes from bentonite, a swelling clay used in foundry, oil drilling, ceramics, insulation, and detergents, among other things. Belle Fourche has four bentonite plants.

There is a uranium plant at Edgemont, and the world's largest mahogany granite quarry is found at Milbank. Much of the city of Sioux Falls is built of the red quartzite in plentiful supply nearby. Well-known pink and buff sandstone quarries are found near Hot Springs.

Farms and Factories

One of the earliest activities in South Dakota was the growing of livestock. Vast herds of cattle grazed the open range. Fortunes were made and sometimes even more quickly lost by blizzard or other disaster. The blizzard of 1886 cost cattlemen the awful total of half of their animals. The blizzard of 1905 ruined most of the cattlemen in the western part of the state.

Corbin Morse owned one of the largest herds. At one time he had 10,000 fine Hereford cattle. He came into Rapid City during a bad blizzard. About an hour later a cowhand staggered through the blizzard to the hotel in Rapid City to tell Morse that the entire herd had stumbled over the cliffs at Big Foot Pass. Half a million dollars worth of the best livestock had perished. Morse's fortune had been wiped out. He paused a moment and said, "Well, easy come, easy go."

At one time Pierre ranked as the greatest point of origin for cattle shipping in the world. The stockyards of Aberdeen still hold position among the leaders in the field. South Dakota ranks among the top ten states in cattle production, with an average of more than 4,000,000 animals.

Sheep raising has long been important in South Dakota. It is said that there are more sheep within a fifty mile radius of Buffalo than in any other similar area of the country. The wool and sheep warehouses of Belle Fourche rank among the leading activities of the community.

Herding sheep is still the same lonesome job it has been since long before the shepherd boy David watched his flocks on the hills. The sheep wagon, equipped as a home on wheels for the shepherd, may have been the original of the modern house trailer. The count of 1964 showed 1,641,000 sheep and lambs in South Dakota.

In the matter of crops, South Dakota has come a long way from the time a farmer from England, named Macy, wrote back to England that he had a 160 acre estate planted entirely in sage. One of the earliest and still the most important crop in South Dakota is hard durum wheat. Eureka was once one of the world's great primary wheat markets. Wheat adds nearly $60,000,000 per year to the state's income.

South Dakota ranks second among the states in the production of rye. Other leading crops are corn, oats, flax and barley. Richest agricultural regions of the state are the James and Sioux river valleys. Land near Forestburg along the James River is especially noted for its melons. Upper Spearfish Valley is renowned for its vegetables, and during the season the Valley road is almost solidly lined with one of the world's great vegetable displays, in neat stands.

Altogether, farm income in South Dakota is more than half a billion dollars each year.

Most manufacturing in South Dakota is based on farm and mineral products such as the bentonite plant of Belle Fourche, and meat packing of Sioux Falls, Watertown and Huron. Manufacturing in the state adds a value of close to $150,000,000 per year.

One of the most unusual activities of South Dakota among all the states was its entry into large-scale manufacturing and commerce in state-owned businesses — the gasoline business, and a cement plant at Rapid City, rural credit and hail insurance. For one reason or another these experiments were all dropped, except for the cement plant.

Electric power is rapidly gaining importance in the state today. One of the few atomic energy plants is the Pathfinder Atomic Power Plant near Sioux Falls, named for John C. Frémont, the Pathfinder. The four giant dams on the Missouri provide the latest important sources of power as well as irrigation and flood control.

Transportation and Communication

Earliest "roads" in what is now South Dakota were the primitive trails such as the old Deadwood Trail out of Pierre, the Bismarck Trail from Bismarck to the Black Hills, and the Cheyenne Trail. One traveler wrote in his diary that he had been on the road for seventeen days by stagecoach between Cheyenne and Custer, ten of these through snowstorms. In addition there was often the danger of stage robberies or Indian attacks.

An unbelievable amount of freight was carried over the early trails in freight wagons, sometimes ponderously drawn by 20 to 40 yoke of oxen. The investment required by such freight business is shown by the fact that oxen might be worth as much as $100 to $150 per yoke.

The rough and stony tracks that forded streams and climbed mountains have been replaced by today's fine modern highways. One of the early promotions of cross-country roads was begun by J. W. Parmley of Ipswich. He originated the idea for the "Yellowstone Trail," now known as United States Highway 12. His ideas have been copied in the promotions for other such highways in various parts of the country. Transcontinental highways 90 (east and west) and 29 (north and south) place South Dakota in good position in the nation's new network of superhighways.

The first convenient transportation in South Dakota came on the rivers, with the Missouri carrying most of the travelers and traders. Most of the river trade of the state centered at Yankton, the railhead after 1872. Fort Pierre was first the head of the wagon road to the Black Hills in 1876-1881 and then the railhead for half a dozen years. As the steamboat age grew, there were forty steamers at one period on the Missouri River; sometimes as many as twenty might be tied up at once in a single port.

Most of this commerce was taken over by the railroads. The first railroad was only a small spur of the Winona and St. Peter Railroad, going to Gary just beyond the state line. Railroad lines reached Sioux Falls in 1878. By 1880 two railroads had built halfway across the state, and there they stopped because of the barrier of the Missouri River.

The first train did not reach Rapid City from across the state until July 10, 1907, when the North Western puffed into town, followed ten days later by the Milwaukee Road. However, Rapid had been connected with the south by rail since 1886. When the first train pulled into Rapid in that year, a touch of the old West was given by a fake stage holdup. It seemed real enough to the passengers, who were not let in on the secret.

First newspaper in what is now South Dakota was the Dakota *Democrat* at Sioux Falls in 1859, soon succeeded by the *Weekly Dakotan*, established at the territorial capital of Yankton in 1861.

53

Human Treasures

Movers of Mountains

Thanks mainly to the determination, inspiration and ability of one man, South Dakota can boast the world's largest work of art, which is also one of the world's most frequently visited. John Gutzon de la Mothe Borglum was born in 1867. By the time he came to South Dakota in the 1920's he was already a renowned sculptor.

When Borglum arrived in the Black Hills, probably not more than ten people believed that anything would ever come of the crazy scheme to make an entire granite mountain into a monument. Few people in the country had even heard of the Black Hills, let alone Mount Rushmore. Even after the work was started hardly anyone would admit that anything like a sculpture would ever appear.

The planning for such a work was monumental in itself. The full ability of the sculptor as an artist went into the making of the design, and then as in almost every sculpture a scale model was made. The skills needed to transform this model into a work of art spread across acres of rock had never before been created.

In his book *Mount Rushmore,* G. C. Fite has described Borglum's work: "The model was first measured by fastening a horizontal bar on the top and center of the head. As this extended out over the face a plumb bob was dropped to the point of the nose, or other projections of the face. Since the model of Washington's face was five feet tall, these measurements were then multiplied by twelve and transferred to the mountain by using a similar but larger device.

"Instead of a small beam, a thirty-foot swinging boom was used, connected to the stone which would ultimately be the top of Washington's head and extending over the granite cliff. A plumb bob was lowered from the boom. The problem was to adjust the measurements from the scale of the model to the mountain.

"The first step was to locate the point of the nose since that was the extreme projection of the face. If it were found that several feet of rock had to be removed to reach the nose point, this was indicated by paint marks. Then other projected points of the face, such as the frontal bones, were located and measured.

"After the rough points were established, men suspended in swing

seats began the drilling and blasting. . . . The blasting was done in such a way as to leave a great rough eggshaped mass. . . .

"It was possible to dynamite within an inch or two of the intended surface, and occasionally this was done at Rushmore. But generally, blasting was not carried on closer than six inches to the surface. . . . Measuring, drilling, blasting, drilling, wedging (splitting), and bumping (smoothing) was the ordinary work cycle. The term 'carving' was only a figure of speech in this gigantic project."

Borglum made Washington's nose an inch too long. This extra length he said would wear away in 100,000 years of erosion. Much the same procedures were followed for the other figures. The work crew did not consist of skilled sculptors but experienced hard-rock miners, trained by Borglum for the work. There was a staff of thirty-six. Nineteen of these operated the compressed-air carving drills. A blacksmith was required to keep all the drilling equipment sharp.

During the fourteen years in which the work went on, innumerable problems came up. Funds grew short until finally the federal government placed the project under the Interior Department. A defect in the rock was discovered where the Jefferson face was to be. The work on Jefferson already done had to be blasted out and the Jefferson face relocated.

The final result has amazed visitors ever since. The rough and wrinkled surface of the uncut rock beside the face of Washington gives a comparison to show how much Borglum accomplished in creating such smooth and polished figures. The tremendous amount of rock cut out is demonstrated by the great pile of rough granite lying up and down the slope of Mount Rushmore.

Many consider the monument as much a monument to its sculptor as it is to the great men it recognizes. However, Borglum modestly insisted that "a monument's dimensions should be determined by the importance to civilization of the events commemorated."

Surprisingly, South Dakota is not only the home of the world's largest monument, but someday also will be the locale of the two largest monuments. Possibly this has come about because, as someone has said, the people of the Black Hills region have the "world's greatest capacity for the unthinkable."

The second project began when Chief Henry Standing Bear told his Sioux fellow councilmen, "I have dreamed of a mountain top memorial like the vast carving on the peak that they now call Rushmore — a picture on a grand scale of our historic leaders, so that the white people may know that the red race had brave men and great men also...."

The council agreed and selected Chief Crazy Horse as the Indian leader to represent them in the sculpture. They invited leading sculptor Korczak Ziolkowski to take charge of the project. Ziolkowski was so impressed with the idea that he found a suitable mountain top and with his own funds bought the mountain and almost 2,000 acres of land. Later someone else claimed the mineral rights to his property, and Ziolkowski had to pay a sort of ransom to this claim jumper to get the right to carve the rock on his land.

The sculptor has designed his impressive model to take advantage of the silhouette of his granite mountain top. With the model placed before it, the mountain in its original form clearly shows the rough outline of the snorting horse and rider outlined in the model. An arm of Crazy Horse rests on his horse's head. The Chief's long hair streams back, in the style Ziolkowski claims was the custom of warriors in battle.

Completion of the sculpture, begun in 1948, is expected to take thirty years, calling for $5,000,000 of chiseling and dynamiting. The sculptor does not want government aid to assist in the work, as aid also imposes direction. The horse will be 400 feet long from tail to nose, and from base to top the statue will be 500 feet high. When completed it will take its place as the world's largest work of art.

Other Creative People

Harvey Dunn was born near DeSmet in a sod house. By the age of fourteen he was using so much chalk in his drawing that the teacher felt compelled to hide it from him. After art study in Chicago, Dunn became an official artist of the War Department during World War I. He gained a reputation as one of the best-known painters of wartime scenes.

David Miller went to the Black Hills in 1935 to capture the character of the local Indians on canvas. He did portraits of more than forty outstanding Indian people, learning the language and customs in order to capture the true Indian character while the tribal life was still largely intact. He came to be known as one of the outstanding artists in this field.

Hamlin Garland spent his formative years on the homestead at Ordway, and he began his writing career there. Much of his writing was based on the people of the Aberdeen region and his experiences there. He once wrote, "Every detail of the daily life on the farm now assumed literary significance in my mind." His first book was *Main Traveled Roads,* written mostly about his neighbors. Others of his well-known books are *Son of the Middle Border,* and *A Daughter of the Middle Border,* for which he won the Pulitzer Prize in biography for 1921.

Ole Edvart Rolvaag gained fame for his realistic novels about Norwegian pioneers in South Dakota. His best known work, *Giants in the Earth,* was based on the lives of the six Berdahl brothers who pioneered in the Canton region. Phil Le Mar Anderson's *Courthouse Square* was also based on the Canton area.

One of the best-known characters of all time was created by L. Frank Baum, who spent his youth in the Aberdeen area. His *Wizard of Oz* is one of the most loved of all creations for children.

Charles Partlon Sale was born in Huron. Writing as "Chic" Sale, his humorous works became very popular, and his *The Specialist* sold over a million copies.

Rose Wilder Lane, popular writer, was born at DeSmet. Those who were familiar with DeSmet easily recognized their community in her book *Old Home Town*. Another regional book was *Sheep,* based on the 16 years sheep-herding experience of Archer B. Gilfallan near Buffalo.

Through the fame of his poems concerning the local scene Badger Clark became known as the Poet Laureate of South Dakota. Other well-known local poets include Jean Wilson Chambers, also a well-known musician, artist and book and magazine illustrator, Dorothy E. Curtis, Dorothy I. Davie, Robert G. Godfrey, Dagney Hinderaker, Corinne Huntington Jackson, Adeline M. Jenney, Phoebe Johnson, Mary Francis Martin, Rhea Smith Meek, Norma L. Olson, Flora Shufelt Rivola, Alma Scheel, Beryl Stewart, E. Talmudge, Enid Thompson, Della B. Vik, Andrae Visser, Thelma Hill Ward, and Allen E. Woodall.

Prominent Tribesmen

The moccasin tracks of Indian leaders have been left deep in South Dakota soil.

One of the best-known of all Indian names is that of the Hunkpapa Sioux Sitting Bull, although he is far from the most admirable of the Indians whose names have gone down in history. Much of his reputation was gained as a medicine man. He did not even fight in the battle of Little Big Horn where "Yellow Hair" (Custer) and his men were massacred. Sitting Bull, supposed Indian leader of that battle, left the fighting to braver men while he stayed in his tepee to "make medicine."

Most authorities agree that Sitting Bull was more a medicine man and politician than a brave. However, there is no question that he wielded great power among his people from his village where Sitting Bull Park is now located.

Chiefs Crazy Horse and Red Cloud were Ogalala Sioux. Crazy Horse was one of the principal Indian leaders in the fight at the battle of Little Big Horn. He surrendered in 1877 but was accused of planning a revolt and was bayoneted in the guard house at Fort Robinson. Red Cloud, leader of the Fetterman Massacre, gained a reputation as one of the several really inspired military geniuses produced by the Indian people. He lived to be 87 years old and died in 1909.

Chief Gabriel Renville became one of the most prominent figures of his region. He was also noted for his three wives and twenty children.

Aces and Eights

General George Armstrong Custer has given an interesting account of James Butler (Wild Bill) Hickok in his book *My Life on the Plains*: "In person he was over six feet one in height, straight as the straightest of the warriors. . . . Add to this figure a costume blending . . . the dandy with the extravagant taste and style of the frontiersman and you have Wild Bill . . . the most famous scout on the plains.

". . . He was one of the most perfect types of physical manhood I ever saw. Of his courage there could be no question. . . . It was entirely free from all bluster or bravado. . . . His conversation, strange to say, never bordered on the vulgar or the blasphemous. His influence on the frontiersmen was unbounded. His word was law. . . . Anything but a quarrelsome man . . . yet I have personal knowledge of at least a dozen men he has killed, including one of my command. . . . There is not a single instance in which the verdict of twelve fair-minded men would not be pronounced in his favor.

"An item lately in the press states: 'The funeral of Jim Bludsoe who was killed the other day by Wild Bill took place today.' It then adds: 'The funeral expenses were borne by Wild Bill.' What could be more thoughtful than this? Not only to send a fellow mortal out of the world but to pay the expenses of the transport."

Time has perhaps dealt somewhat more kindly with Martha Jane Canary than she deserves. Known as Calamity Jane, she first came to the Black Hills in 1876. Later she left for 17 years and returned to spend most of the remainder of her life there. There have been many differing estimates of her character. However, she has become a legendary figure, and South Dakota prefers to remember the interesting and colorful parts of her life rather than any human weaknesses she may have had.

Poker-Alice Tubbs, of Sturgis, noted for her skill at the game and for her cigar smoking, was another of the noted women of the wild West.

The name "Deadwood Dick" was made famous in the cheap novels of the late 1800's. This fiction did much to spread the fame of the Black Hills country. The character may have been based on the life of Richard Clark, supposed to have driven the first stage into Deadwood. In any event, in recent years a Richard Clark took over the title. He received so much attention and publicity as Deadwood Dick that some writers say he came to believe that he really was the original. His funeral was larger than the one for Wild Bill Hickok.

The first minister in the Black Hills was the Rev. Henry Weston Smith, given the colorful name of Preacher Smith. He became much loved by the people of the region, and when he was killed by Indians, the area mourned one of its few humanitarians.

Such Interesting People

Alex C. Johnson was one of the principal promoters of the Black Hills and of Rapid City. He also was one of the leaders in the move to make Pierre the state capital. As vice president in charge of operations for the North Western Railroad, Mr. Johnson had one of the most colorful careers of his time. He retired to the Alex Johnson Hotel in Rapid City, named in his honor.

Peter Norbeck, who gained his greatest public attention as Senator from South Dakota, was one of the country's leading conservationists. He was another of the great promoters of the Black Hills. The *South Dakota Guide* records, "While the fine Needles highway was being built, the late Sen. Peter Norbeck tramped on foot over every mile of this rough country and whenever he found a particularly striking view, he would say to the engineers, 'Run the road here.' They would assure him that it was impossible, to which he would reply, 'Put it there anyway.' And they did. This man did more than any other to make the natural beauties of the Black Hills region available and accessible to all."

Another public figure, Governor William A. Howard, gained particular fame by using his own funds to provide a place for the insane at Yankton. Yet another who achieved far greater public attention was Fiorello H. La Guardia, colorful mayor of New York City, whose youth, by contrast, was spent in the small community of Fort Sully.

Richard Sears, founder of Sears and Roebuck, is said to have gotten his start in Wolsey. At that town, he was so successful in selling a shipment of unclaimed watches for the owners that he began a small mail order business. After two years he left Wolsey, and his business eventually mushroomed into the world's largest retail establishment.

One of the most interesting true sagas of the old West was that of Hugh Glass. He was a guide for the William Ashley party in 1823 when he was attacked by a grizzly bear. Ashley left the unconscious Glass in care of two of his men, who decided he was dead and deserted him. Regaining consciousness, Glass, terribly mangled, made his way the incredible distance of a hundred and seventy miles across the prairie to Fort Kiowa on the Missouri River.

As soon as he had recovered, Glass set out to overtake and punish the two men who had left him. After many more hardships, he finally found them both but forgave them, in an action which one writer says "raises his story to the level of sublimity."

James "Scotty" Philip, one of the largest ranchers of the state, gained the nickname of the "Buffalo King." In order to preserve the fast-dying buffalo, he bought the small Dupois herd and at his death the herd had grown to more than 1,000. Some say that he kept the buffalo herd to please his Indian wife, who was very sad that they had almost died out. When Philip died, as his body was taken from his home to a nearby Paiute cemetery, the entire herd, on its way to water, filed silently by.

Samuel J. Brown, chief of scouts at Fort Sisseton, gained fame by a horseback ride of 135 miles, mostly through a blizzard, to undo a warning he had erroneously given and avoid possible bloodshed. After the ride Brown was paralyzed for the remainder of his life.

Corbin Morse gained fame for the unusual home he built near Rapid City and for his entertaining. Almost every famous person to come to the region was entertained at the Morse home, including Theodore Roosevelt, William Jennings Bryan, Jim Corbett, May Irwin, Lillian Russell, Cy Young, and Mark Twain.

Earle Sande, noted jockey, was a native of Groton. John Robertson was noted for improving the native fruits. A. C. McDonald contributed to the fame of his state by developing Wind Cave. Another who brought publicity was George Bronson, who helped to bring the stratosphere flight to the Hills.

Teaching and Learning

Founded in 1881, Yankton College is the oldest college in the Dakotas. Today's sixteen institutions of higher learning in the state include seven state colleges and the university, six four-year colleges and three junior colleges.

The University of South Dakota had one of the most unusual beginnings of all the state universities. The territorial legislature of 1862 established the university but provided no funds for it. In 1882 the people of Vermillion decided to open the state university themselves. Judge Jefferson Kidder donated ten acres of land, and the county provided $10,000 through a bond issue, to build the first building, not completed when classes began in 1882. The community of Vermillion carried on the state university for a year before the legislature appropriated the first funds.

Although one of the smaller state universities, the University of South Dakota has made a significant contribution to the growth and culture of the area.

CAMPANILE, SOUTH DAKOTA STATE COLLEGE

Almost equally important has been the contribution of the South Dakota State College begun at Brookings in 1883, now having a slightly larger enrollment than the university. Particularly significant has been the work of the state college in agriculture, including such renowned efforts as Professor James Wilson's development of a much desired breed of tailless sheep. The well-known Agricultural Experiment Station is near the campus. Here the latest advances are developed for farmers throughout the state and their problems are carefully studied.

One of the leading institutions of its kind is the South Dakota School of Mines and Technology at Rapid City, founded in 1885. Although the work in mining has been especially outstanding, the school carries on activities of a full-fledged technological institution. The college's Institute of Atmospheric Sciences conducts research on how it may be possible to change weather in the future. The School of Mines Sheep Mountain Camp provides noteworthy work in paleontology.

The first of South Dakota's teachers' colleges was Eastern State Normal School, begun at Madison in 1883. It is now known as General Beadle State Teachers College.

Among the outstanding private colleges of the state are Dakota Wesleyan University at Mitchell, Augustana College and Sioux Falls College at Sioux Falls, and Huron College at Huron.

In the field of public education, South Dakota educators developed a new method of teaching which has been widely adopted throughout the world. This was started at Aberdeen and has come to be known by educators as the "Aberdeen Plan." This is usually considered the "invention" of what is now called "Cooperative Education," where part of the student's course is actual on-the-job work, supervised by the school.

First school in South Dakota was begun with great sacrifice by the people of Bon Homme County in 1860. They built a log building with a dirt floor where ten pupils attended the first term, lasting three months. Then as now the people of South Dakota were convinced that no community was complete without the best education it was possible to provide.

Enchantment of South Dakota

Few states offer to visitors the extraordinary contrasts of South Dakota. There are some of the best farmlands, with good natural rainfall, arid, almost desert lands, some of them now watered by great artificial lakes, and some of the country's finest forested mountain land. Throughout the state the visitor is apt to find many unexpected delights as well as some of the outstanding attractions in the country.

Gateway to the Hills — Rapid City

Rapid City, a boom town when it was founded in 1876, and still a boom town today, is a rapidly growing center, far more metropolitan than its population might indicate.

Visitors who approach Rapid City probably will see first the city's trademarks — the concrete prehistoric monsters of famed Dinosaur Park on top of Skyline Ridge. Largest of these carefully reproduced life-sized animals is the huge brontosaurus, visible as far away as forty miles. Dinosaur Park, this unusual attraction of the city, was first proposed by Dr. O'Harra, then president of the State School of Mines.

Remains of real dinosaurs found so plentifully in the state may be seen in the school's Museum of Geology, one of the country's outstanding displays of fossils, minerals and other materials of geology. Exhibits of mammal life from the Badlands are said to be the finest of their kind anywhere.

Another of the city's museums is Sioux Museum, containing what is probably the most complete collection of materials on the Sioux tribes. The collection includes many especially rare items of this nature as well as some striking dioramas.

Three commercial displays and museums include Marine Life, a porpoise and seal show, with other marine displays, the Reptile Gardens where large varieties of snakes are shown in simulations of their native habitats, and the Horseless Carriage Museum, a collection of old autos and other mechanical devices.

Storybook Island is the community's playground for its young people. Playground attractions are made to represent various children's stories, such as the *Old Woman Who Lived in a Shoe*.

The city first gained fame as home of the summer White House in 1927, when Calvin Coolidge used the Rapid High School as his office, driving to work every day from the State Game Lodge where he lived. Now visitors recognize that Rapid is convenient to all the other places of interest in the Black Hills region, giving it the nickname of Gateway to the Black Hills. Interesting rides out of the city include scenic Rim Rock Trail, South Canyon, a deep tree-shaded gorge, and Rapid Canyon, said to have more interest for geologists than any other area in the Hills.

Gulch of the Dead Wood

Deadwood is a frontier town that refused to die as so many of them did. Chambers Keller, a Homestake Mine lawyer, once said, "There isn't any doubt that Deadwood is one of the most interesting towns in America. I don't know of any other place where you are so conscious of the past while living in so modern a present. The reason for that is that the town was built well and adequately to begin with. . . . Except for one or two buildings it is exactly the same town physically that it was in the eighties. . . . There is one western town that can put on any pageant it likes without having to worry about whether or not it looks authentic."

Because of its location in the gulch, Deadwood is a town of only one main street. Its liveliest time comes during the annual "Days of '76," when there is a rodeo and the early days are re-enacted. Deadwood

remembers its past when flour was $60 a barrel, when a miner might scatter golden nuggets on the street just to see the people scramble for them, where early religious services were held in the Melodeon gambling house and saloon because there was no other place for them.

One of the favorite Deadwood stories tells how Slippery Sam and Charlie the Bartender had a fight one night in the Bella Union bar. Charlie threw Sam out and told him he would shoot him if he ever came back. Sam found a character named Bummer Dan, gave Dan his overcoat and asked him to go and collect a dollar that Charlie the Bartender owed to Sam. Seeing Sam's overcoat on Dan, Charlie shot him. With strange logic, the jury acquitted Charlie because he had shot the wrong man.

Memories of those early days are preserved in the Adams Memorial Museum at Deadwood, founded by W. E. Adams. The unique exhibits include a letter from Wovoka, the Messiah, Indian saddles, a collection of early photographs of Deadwood, the first locomotive in the Hills, a record of gold being found in the Hills as early as 1834, and many other items.

Most visitors to Deadwood make their way to Mt. Moriah Cemetery, Deadwood's "boot hill." There are the graves of Wild Bill Hickok, Calamity Jane and others. The statue of Wild Bill has had to be replaced twice because souvenir hunters have chipped it away, bit by bit.

Near Deadwood is Mount Roosevelt, from which four states can be seen. On the mountain is a memorial to Theodore Roosevelt, commemorating his visit to the region. The Deadwood Hill drive is considered one of the most outstanding in the Hills.

Other Hill Towns

An annual drama has made Spearfish one of the nation's well-known towns. Josef Meier had played Christus in the Passion Play of Lunen, Germany. When he fled from Germany after Hitler came to power, he brought the Lunen Passion Play to America and presented it in many cities.

After they gave the play in Spearfish, Guy Bell of Spearfish asked them to make Spearfish the permanent home of the Passion Play so that Spearfish might have a really worthwhile attraction for visitors. The Black Hills Passion Play has been bringing the dignity of its great message to the Black Hills region ever since, except during World War II, playing to reverent throngs.

Another dramatic attraction of the Hills is the Black Hills Playhouse, near Legion Lake.

One of the attractions of the Spearfish region is the large Federal Fish Hatcheries which stock the many streams with trout. Spearfish Canyon is known as one of the nation's loveliest.

Belle Fourche, one of the economic centers of the Black Hills region, is noted for its annual Black Hills Roundup, one of the country's leading rodeos.

At one time Sturgis was known as "Scoop Town" because the soldiers from nearby Fort Meade were so often "scooped" or cleaned out by clever poker players such as Poker-Alice Tubbs, the cigar-smoking woman scoop expert. Another early memory of Sturgis is preserved by the monument at Dead Man Creek. Charles Nolin was the "Dead Man" of the Creek's name. He was a pony mail carrier killed by the Indians at that place. Shading the Nolin memorial are five black walnut trees, grown from slips taken from five historic battlefields, including Valley Forge, Antietam, and Gettysburg.

Historic Fort Meade no longer hears the thundering hoofs of its western cavalry. It is now a veterans hospital. One of the unusual stories of the fort is that the only survivor of Custer's troops in the battle of Little Big Horn was brought to Fort Meade and lived there for many years. This was the horse, Comanche.

Near Sturgis is Bear Butte, a batholith of granite rising from the level ground to a height of 4,422 feet. This was one of the most sacred shrines of the Indians, and it was customary for them to make an

annual pilgrimage to its slopes. The region is now known as Bear Butte State Park.

While Deadwood is crowded into the bottom of its gulch, its neighbor Lead (pronounced Leed) spreads out across the head of Gold Run Gulch at a mile-high level. Neither town has any level ground, but if possible, Lead is hillier than Deadwood.

The yawning cavern of the Homestake Mine's open cut is the most striking thing about Lead. The mine has regular tours showing the surface workings and explaining methods of gold production and refining to interested visitors.

Some of the country's most dramatic views may be had from the Terry Peak ski lift near Lead. This 4,000 foot long chair lift dangles the visitor far above the dark green landscape for a dramatic view of mountain wonderland from the second highest mountain in the Black Hills. The region is also tops for winter sports.

Custer, of course, is where it all began — where General Custer's force found gold, where the first horde of goldseekers came, and the first community began in the Black Hills. Today's population is a long way from the ten or fifteen thousand who arrived in the early days, but it is a good deal larger than it was when most of the people left Custer almost overnight to rush to the gold of the northern Hills.

Custer remembers the early days with one of the nation's leading annual pageants — Gold Discovery Days. This has been called the "most fascinating thing of its type in the Hills."

The Log Cabin Museum at Custer has an interesting display of pioneer, historical and mineral exhibits.

Hot Springs was first settled in 1879. At one time it held much the same position as Reno, Nevada, today. Quick divorces were possible in South Dakota in the early 1900's, and people came to Hot Springs to rid themselves of their husbands or wives and their aches and pains at the same time.

Today, with the quick divorce laws long since changed, the mineral springs are still popular tourist attractions. The Evans Plunge offers the largest natural indoor warm water pool in the world. The life of the Sioux warrior is remembered each year in the Crazy Horse Pageant given each night during the summer.

The Treasures of Paha Sapa

The modern treasures of Paha Sapa, the Indian name for the Black Hills, are far more than the gold. The tourist, in fact, is more apt to find his gold mine in the sky when the aspen turn in autumn. The other modern treasures of the Hills consist of a varied collection of

THE NEEDLES

wonders and attractions possibly larger than can be found anywhere else in so small an area.

One of the Hill's most interesting natural wonders is the unique Needles formation. These "glorious granite spires" are gigantic spears of rock jutting toward the sky — the eroded remnants of the aged granite core of the Hills. In one of the needles is a hole, which, of course, has been named the Needle's Eye.

Dotted around the Hills are many serene lakes, of which the best known is the tranquil beauty of tiny Sylvan Lake, clutched in a granite bowl, close to Harney Peak. Another tranquil beauty is Stockade Lake; here is a monument in memory of Annie D. Tallant, first woman in the Black Hills.

The rugged peaks of the mountains lure many visitors to their summits. There is a jeep ride up Harney Peak, highest point in the state. This mountain is driven or climbed each year by thousands of people. The rangers say that almost every visitor asks if they "don't get lonesome up there." The road to the top of 7,172 foot Bear Mountain is also popular, and the road up Mount Coolidge is said to be one of the most picturesque in the state. One of the best views of the region is had from the top of Custer Peak.

Wind Cave, established in 1903 as a national park, is the only national park in South Dakota. It takes its name from the currents of air that rush in and out as the barometric pressure changes. The whistling sound of air led to its discovery in 1881. The only natural entrance was an opening ten inches across.

Jewel Cave, west of Custer, is a national monument. It has some of the finest displays of natural crystals anywhere, enchanting visitors as they catch the light and sparkle brilliantly. Crystal Cave near Piedmont is another cave lined with brilliant gem-like crystals.

Custer State Park with 128,000 acres is the second largest state park in the United States. Biggest attraction is the buffalo herd. Visitors are taken on a jeep ride through the herd, and there is an annual buffalo roundup in July. There is a zoo and museum in the park.

Visitors are enchanted by the glorious scenery along the narrow-gauge tracks as they chug along in a steam train of the 1880 period on one of the few rides of its kind still available — from Hill City to Keystone. Other picturesque and scenic trips through the Black Hills are those through Fall River and Boulder canyons.

Although possibly twenty years of work still remain on the Crazy Horse Memorial, visitors flock to see the work as it stands. Already more than five times the amount of rock removed from Mount Rushmore has been removed here.

Sculptor Korczak Ziolkowski intends the monument to honor not only Crazy Horse and the Indian people but also what he calls the "unconquerable spirit of man" in general. Ziolkowski hopes to have a great Indian center at the foot of the memorial, including a university, historical museum and hospital.

Climax of almost any visit in the Black Hills is the visit to Mount Rushmore, viewed by about 1,500,000 people each year. Charles E. Rushmore visited the Keystone region in the 1880's. He made many friends. One day while walking with a friend in the mountains he asked the name of one peak and was told that it was called Rushmore. Elated and gullible, he told about it on returning to the boarding house. The old sourdoughs knew a joke when they heard it and did not contradict him. He left thinking the peak really was called Rushmore. Those who were in on the joke began to call it by that name in jest, and the name stuck. So it was that a "joke mountain" by an odd twist of fate became one of the best known in the world and an unwitting memorial to Lawyer Rushmore.

In his incomparable patriotic work on Rushmore, sculptor Gutzon Borglum chose George Washington to represent the founding of the Union, Thomas Jefferson to represent the country's expansion, Abraham Lincoln to represent the preservation of the Union, and Theodore Roosevelt the modern development of the United States.

Today, as visitors view these "immortals of Rushmore," especially as the floodlights of night pick out their strong features, most of them go away with a little better understanding of just what their country means to them and to the world.

Mako Sico — Bad Lands

No other region of the world is quite like the region now called the Badlands National Monument. Dr. Cleophas C. O'Harra, of the South

Dakota School of Mines, once described the fantastic formations as being like "Magnificent ruins of a great silent city painted in delicate shades of cream and pink and buff and green! Domes, towers, minarets, and spires decorate gorgeous cathedrals and palaces. At first there may come a feeling of the incongruous or grotesque, but studying more closely the meaning of every feature, the spirit of this marvelous handiwork of the Great Creator develops in vistas of beauty. . . ."

The great architect, Frank Lloyd Wright, wrote of the Badlands: "As we rode, or seemed to be floating upon a splendid winding road . . . we rose and fell between its delicate parallels of rose and cream and sublime shapes, chalk white, fretted against a blue sky, with high floating clouds. . . . Communion with what man often calls 'God' is inevitable in this place."

President Franklin D. Roosevelt made the region a National Monument in 1939; headquarters are at Cedar Pass.

Near Interior is the only sand crystal bed on the North American Continent. These unique crystals are shaped like plumbing pipes, from a quarter of an inch to fifteen inches long. They are found in the sandy soil of the sand crystal bed which for some reason remains moist in this dry region. When first dug up, the crystals break easily, but after exposure to air they harden into grotesque shapes.

Close to the east entrance of the Badlands National Monument is Prairie Homestead Historical Site. This is particularly noteworthy because it shows a typical sod dugout homestead in the original location, furnished as if the homestead family were still living there.

Pierre of the Realm

Most states think a central state capital is desirable, but few have achieved this as well as South Dakota. The geographical center of the state is five miles north of Pierre (pronounced Peer). Pierre claims to be the "meeting place of East and West," and also claims to be the only city on the Missouri River that owns all of its own waterfront.

Pierre is also the center for the vast new world of lakes created in South Dakota. Oahe Dam is only six miles north of the city. This is the largest rolled earth dam in the world and the greatest of all the Missouri River basin projects.

The state capitol, dedicated in 1910, cost a million dollars, and is an especially impressive achievement for a state of such small population.

One of the most valuable historical mementoes of the state is the famed Vérendrye plate, buried by the exploring brothers. This is now exhibited in the South Dakota Historical Museum, as are many other historical and Indian mementoes.

At another historic spot — Fort Pierre across the river — a monument to the Vérendryes has been placed on Vérendrye Hill. Here also is a map of South Dakota, made by members of the Young Citizens League from stones collected from each county of the state.

North of Farm Island State Park on Hipple Lake was the location of old Fort Sully. A monument on the island recalls the visit of Lewis and Clark on their historic journey.

The Pierre region is noted for its granite glacier boulders — the only ones of their kind west of St. Cloud, Minnesota. These mark the westernmost drift of the great glaciers.

The Northern Slice

The vast northwestern corner of South Dakota is a land of silences, endless open distances, and sometimes of majestic beauty. Here is found a large part of the world's petrified wood. At Petrified Wood Park near Lemmon the buildings are made of petrified wood. The Short Pine Hills and Slim Buttes, a "monumental escarpment," are little-known areas of real charm. Reva Gap presents an unexpected view of scenery and odd rock formations, and Summit Pass near Reva Gap offers a magnificent view of typical prairie scenery. The mud buttes near Redig and the gumbo country near Castle Rock have their own strange attractions.

In 1907 the Milwaukee Railroad built a bridge across the Missouri

River, and the telegraph operator there signed his messages as Mo. Bridge to show his location at the Missouri bridge. The town that grew up there took the abbreviation for its name — Mobridge.

To the west across the river is a region of many memories of Arikara and Sioux Indians. Both tribes had villages there, with the Sioux finally driving the Arikara out. The region is especially well known for its associations with Sitting Bull. That well-publicized medicine man-chief had his headquarters village near Little Eagle. His home site, now known as Sitting Bull Park, has been preserved as it was when he fell. The grave of Sitting Bull with its monument occupies a high rise across the river from Mobridge, giving a spectacular view of the town and surrounding region. Here the crafty leader finds a peace never known in his lifetime.

Nearby is the monument to Sacajawea, respected and famed Shoshone Indian guide of the Lewis and Clark party. Known as the Bird Woman, she was the wife of a French trapper named Charbonneau. A Shoshone wife of Charbonneau died and was buried at Fort Manuel near this site, and all collateral evidence is that this was truly Sacajawea who was buried there. Fort Manuel was destroyed during the War of 1812; it was later reconstructed and archeologists have recently studied the site.

A monument to Indian soldiers who gave their lives during World War I is located at Little Eagle, and it was here that the Sioux revived their rain dance in 1936 during the terrible drought of that period.

Four railroads make Aberdeen a transportation center. Television stations, Northern State Teachers College, zoo, baseball farm club of the Baltimore Orioles, and wholesale and other commercial activities make Aberdeen a much more metropolitan center than might be imagined from its population of about 25,000.

In early days the settlers planted the bare prairies with thousands of trees, making Aberdeen today a forested community. The drug store of Hamlin Garland's *Main Traveled Roads* was located in Aberdeen.

Some of the grandeur of old Fort Sisseton has been restored. For many years this was the leading cultural center of a whole vast region. Later the fort was bought by Colonel W. C. Boyce, who used it as a lavish private estate for several years.

Watertown is a prosperous manufacturing community, noted for its recreation around Lake Kampeska. The home of South Dakota's first governor has been restored there. This was Arthur Mellette, the unselfish public official who turned over his complete fortune to help repair the losses caused by the alleged dishonesty of the state treasurer. The "state capitol" building built by businessmen to lure the capital to Watertown was never used for its intended purpose. Later it became a night club.

FORT SISSETON

The Southeast

Chamberlain is heaquarters for visits to the Crow Creek and Lower Brule Indian reservations. A trading post, Fort Aux Cedras, was built at American Island as early as 1809.

Plankinton held a grain festival in 1891. The event was remembered mainly because the festival featured a corn palace. This preceded the Corn Palace which has made the name of Mitchell known throughout the world. This famed building was first built in 1892 and has been rebuilt twice, most recently at a cost of $300,000; it now seats 5,000. However, it is known mainly for the fact that each year its outside is covered with corn and grasses. Extraordinary murals are created using

only countless colored seeds of corn and other grain and decorative grasses. The work has been designed and supervised for many years by Oscar Howe, artist laureate of the state.

The Corn Palace Festival is a colorful six-day affair which has attracted many celebrities and always features big-name entertainers, beginning in 1904 with John Philip Sousa.

The museum at Mitchell displays exhibits of the nearby Arikara Village site. Mitchell had been started on another site, but a railroad expert sent to locate a town picked up a piece of driftwood where the first town had started. "No town should be built here," he declared. "If water has flooded here and brought in driftwood it will do it again." So Mitchell was located at its present site and sure enough, the old town was completely covered in a flood two years afterward.

Huron bills itself as the "Pheasant Capital of the World." It boosts this reputation with the "world's largest pheasant" — a forty-foot high monster of steel and glass fiber, weighing 22 tons. Huron is the site of the South Dakota State Fair, where the State Fair Pioneer Museum is located.

The Legia Greischa Colony near Arlington was established as a Swiss communal center; here all property was owned in common. As soon as the residents were financially able, they abandoned the cooperative arrangement.

Brookings is dominated by its vital State College community. One of the state's outstanding structures is the 165 foot Coughlin Campanile and chimes, a gift of Charles L. Coughlin. It harmonizes with the nearby Coolidge Sylvan Theater and Lincoln Memorial Library. The College Union is noted for its collection of the famed paintings of South Dakota artist Harvey Dunn, who specialized in war scenes.

The region north and east of Sioux Falls is renowned for its scenery. At the picturesque Dells of the Big Sioux River the swift current has cut deep gorges near Dell Rapids. The Palisades State Recreation Area features a beautiful pink and purple gorge of jasper rock. Devil's Gulch, near Garretson, is a jagged gash in the prairie where there is said to be a "bottomless pit." Garretson was noted for its annual roly-poly tournament, a sport similar to horseshoes but played with wooden disks which are rolled.

SOKOL FESTIVAL
DURING CZECH DAYS

Baltic, known as Little Norway, is prominent for its annual enactment of a Norwegian Hardanger, a traditional wedding festival. The Sioux Valley Ski Slide gained fame from the national ski tournament held there every five years. Jefferson was the home of the first Catholic church in the state, begun in 1867.

Vermillion is the site of the University of South Dakota. The university's W. H. Over Museum has an extraordinary collection of relics of Indians and natural history specimens.

Historic Yankton has restored the Territorial Council Chamber where meetings of the Dakotas' legislature were held. Another historic institution is Yankton College, first college in the Dakotas. Mighty Gavin's Point Dam is reached by following historic Fort Randall Military Road. The city is especially prominent for its 130 foot wide streets, pleasant boulevards lined with flowers and shrubs.

Tabor attracts many visitors with the rollicking fun of its Czech Days. The Sokol Festival there features the traditional Sokol or setting up exercises of the Czechoslovakian homeland.

84

Where Falls the Sioux

The Big Sioux River cascades over a series of impressive waterfalls. French explorer Jean Nicolas Nicollet wrote a striking description of them. In 1856 Dr. George M. Staples of Dubuque, Iowa, was so impressed with the Nicollet description of the site that he formed the Western Town Company of Dubuque to establish a settlement where the Sioux went over its falls. The Dakota Land Company was organized in Minnesota for the same purpose.

Settlement began by both rival companies working harmoniously, and by 1858 there were thirty or forty residents. In the election of that year they appointed each other election clerks and set out across the countryside in groups of three or four. Every few miles they stopped, established an election precinct and cast their votes and the votes of all their relatives. Several hundred "votes" were cast in an effort to impress federal authorities.

During the Indian uprising of 1862, Sioux Falls was abandoned, and the Indians used type from the local press to make decorations for their

pipes and other articles. However, the settlement resumed in 1868, and since that time Sioux Falls has grown to become the largest city in the state. During the first decade of the 1900's, its growth took an interesting turn. Because of the easy divorce laws and because it was easy to reach, Sioux Falls became a quickie divorce center. Among the well-known people who came to the city for a divorce was Mrs. Bob Fitzsimmons, wife of the heavyweight boxing champion.

He went to Sioux Falls and talked his wife out of the divorce. Highly pleased, Fitzsimmons went to the local blacksmith shop to celebrate by forging horse shoes and giving them to his local admirers. So many crowded into the shop that the old floors gave way, and they all dropped into the basement with a thud. Only one boy was hurt, Fitzsimmons staged a benefit the next day, raised $250 for the boy's expenses, and gave the rest of the money to the Children's Home.

Today the city is a center of diversified industry, a prosperous farming region, and commercial center of a wide area. The Pathfinder Atomic Energy Power Plant — the only completely atomic power plant in the country — was completed in 1962, and guided tours are open. The Pettigrew Museum has a good collection of Indian materials, historical and natural history exhibits. The Great Plains Zoo specializes in animals of the region and does this most effectively. The summer theater at Sioux Falls provides many varied and outstanding offerings.

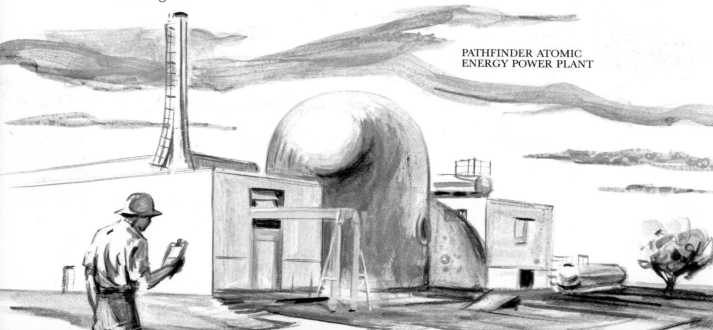

PATHFINDER ATOMIC
ENERGY POWER PLANT

FALLS PARK, SIOUX FALLS

At Falls Park, the roaring Big Sioux still thunders with the cascade that so impressed scientist Nicolas Nicollet. Terrace Park has an interesting novelty. Here a lake is stocked with fish and reserved entirely for fishing by children.

Augustana College, established in 1889, provides prominent higher educational facilities for the region. The Catholic Cathedral of St. Joseph is one of the most impressive buildings in the state.

The Industrial Development Expansion Agency of South Dakota has said that "when the prairie schooners of the pioneer rolled out of the woods upon the vast reaches of land of this region, it was like a gateway opening on a new world. . . . The feeling lingers until this day. . . . The blending of past and present is woven into a tapestry of interest and delight, loomed upon the foundations of America."

Handy Reference Section

Instant Facts

Became the 39th or 40th state (see text for explanation) November 2, 1889

Capital — Pierre, settled 1880

State Bird — Ring-necked Pheasant

State Flower — Pasqueflower (pulsatilla ludoviciana)

State Tree — Black Hills Spruce

State Gem Stone — Rose Quartz

State Animal — Coyote

State Motto — Under God the People Rule

State Song — "Hail, South Dakota"

Area — 77,047 square miles

Area Rank — 16th

Greatest Length (north to south) — 210 miles

Greatest Width (east to west) — 370 miles

Highest Point — 7,242 feet (Harney Peak)

Lowest Point — 965 feet, northeast corner at Big Stone Lake

Geographical Center — north of Pierre

Highest Recorded Temperature — 120° (Gannvalley)

Lowest Recorded Temperature — minus 58° (McIntosh)

Population — 721,000 (1965 estimate)

Population Density — 8.9 persons per square mile (1960 census)

Principal Cities		
Sioux Falls —	65,466	(1960)
Rapid City —	42,399	
Aberdeen —	23,073	
Huron —	14,180	
Watertown —	14,077	

You Have a Date with History

1743 Vérendrye brothers claim region for King of France
1750 Sioux invasion begins
1780 Pierre Dorion becomes first white settler
1794 Jean Baptiste Trudeau establishes trading post in present Charles Mix County
1803 United States purchases Louisiana Territory
1804 Lewis and Clark reach present South Dakota
1811 Wilson Price Hunt party traverses region
1817 First permanent settlement, later known as Fort Pierre
1823 Indians attack Ashley party
1833 American Fur Company trading post built near Vermillion
1838 John C. Frémont explores
1848 Father Pierre DeSmet visits
1856 Sioux Falls founded
1861 Dakota Territory created
1864 Fort Sisseton established
1874 Custer expedition discovers Black Hills gold
1880 Worst winter on record
1889 Statehood
1890 South Dakota site of last United States-Indian battle
1898 Ring-necked pheasant introduced
1903 Wind Cave made a National Park
1904 Pierre becomes permanent capital
1927 President Coolidge visits South Dakota
1935 *Explorer II* breaks altitude mark
1939 Badlands made National Monument
1941 Final drilling at Mount Rushmore
1949 South Dakota becomes nation's leading gold producer
1962 First all-nuclear power plant completed at Sioux Falls

Annual Events

January — S. D. Snow Queen Festival, Aberdeen
May — All-College Rodeo, Brookings
June — State Rock Show, Hot Springs
June — Czech Days, Tabor
June — Gala Days, Bison
June-August — Black Hills Passion Play, Spearfish
June-August — Crazy Horse Pageant, Hot Springs
July — Sitting Bull Stampede, Mobridge
July — Sioux Tribal Celebration, Sisseton
July — Black Hills Roundup, Belle Fourche
July — Gold Discovery Days Rodeo and Pageant, Custer
August — Ft. Randall Pow-Wow, Lake Andes
August — Days of '76, Deadwood
August — Black Hills Motor Classic, Sturgis
August — Frontier Days Rodeo, White River
August — Black Hills Range Days Rodeo, Rapid City
August — Little World Series, Aberdeen
September — Corn Palace Festival, Mitchell

Thinkers, Doers, Fighters

People of renown who have been associated with South Dakota

Baum, L. Frank
Big Foot (Chief)
Borglum, John Gutzon de la Mothe
Borglum, Lincoln
Chambers, Jean Wilson
Crazy Horse (Chief)
Dunn, Harvey
Garland, Hamlin
Johnson, Alex C.
La Guardia, Fiorello H.
Lane, Rose Wilder
Mellette, Arthur C.
Norbeck, Peter
Red Cloud (Chief)
Rolvaag, Ole Edvart
Sale, Charles Partlon (Chic)
Sande, Earle
Sitting Bull (Chief)
Ziolkowski, Korczak

Governors of the State of South Dakota

Arthur C. Mellette   1889-93
Charles H. Sheldon   1893-97
Andrew F. Lee   1897-01
Charles N. Herried   1901-05
Samuel H. Elrod   1905-07
Coe I. Crawford   1907-09
Robert S. Vessey   1909-13
Frank M. Byrne   1913-17
Peter Norbeck   1917-21
William H. McMaster   1921-25
Carl Gunderson   1925-27
William J. Bulow   1927-31

Warren H. Green   1931-33
Tom Berry   1933-37
Leslie Jensen   1937-39
Harlan J. Bushfield   1939-43
M. Q. Sharpe   1943-47
George Mickelson   1947-51
Sigurd Abderson   1951-55
Joe Foss   1955-59
Ralph Herseth   1959-61
Archie Gubbrud   1961-65
Nils A. Boe   1965-

INDEX

93

About the Author: Allan Carpenter was born in Waterloo, Iowa. He went to Iowa State College and then taught at the Des Moines Junior High School and at Drake University. He left teaching to found the magazine *Teachers' Digest* which he published for eight years. He has been associated with publishing for many years and now works full time as a free-lance writer. His first book was published when he was 20 and since then he has written over fifty books.

———

About the Illustrator: Roger Herrington grew up in Sault Ste. Marie, Michigan, on the American side of the Soo Locks. His stepfather was a tugboat captain which took the family to many parts of the United States. While he was in college, Roger worked during summers as a boatman on the Erie Canal. He went to the American Academy of Art in Chicago for his art training, and spent two years at the Ringling School of Art in Sarasota, Florida. He now has his own studio in Chicago and devotes most of his working time to illustrating books.